LENNOX

Photographs Blaise Hart
Text Melissa Mathison

Little, Brown

A Little, Brown Book

First published in Great Britain in 2002 by Little, Brown

Copyright © Dryfleet Limited 2002

The right of Melissa Mathison to be identified as Author of this Work has been asserted by her in accordance with the Copyright, Designs and Patents Act 1988.

A CIP catalogue record for this book is available from the British Library.

ISBN 0-316-85786-6

Designed by Brian Wall

Printed and bound in Great Britain by Butler and Tanner Ltd

Little, Brown
An imprint of Time Warner Books UK
Brettenham House
Lancaster Place
London WC2E 7EN

www.TimeWarnerBooks.co.uk

www.lennoxlewis.com

Contents

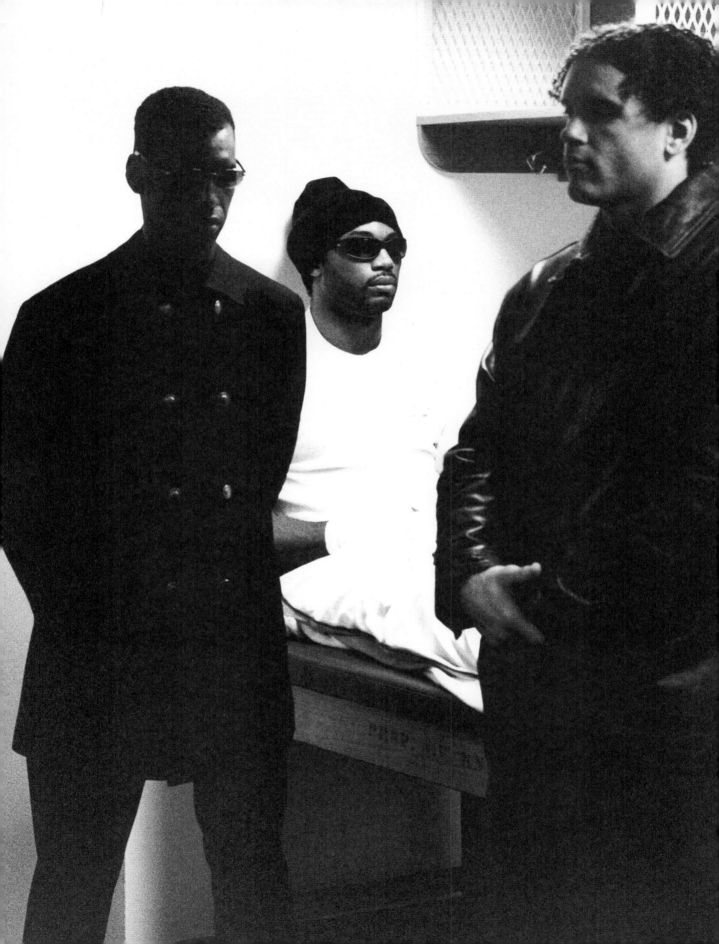

Brutal?

Yes ...

and no.

Introduction

Lennox Claudius Lewis.

Born September 2 1965. London, England. He was so big, the doctor said to his mother, Violet, 'You've got a real Lennox!' And so, she named him. I've been searching for some definition of 'Lennox' – a tall glass of water, big kahuna, fat boy – and find nothing. I think the doctor might have said 'lummox'. Lummox Lewis? No way.

It's *Lennox* Lewis.

6 feet, 5 inches, last weighed in at 246 pounds. He has an 84-inch reach from one fingertip pointed west to the other fingertip pointed east. He has three – not two, not one – muscle creases in his calves. He's got a little gray hair at the temples and a few scattered across his chest – 'platinum', he calls them. He wears his hair long, in twists. He sews it up when he fights, and yes, he's got a bit of a Samson thing going on. He likes to drive fast, eat heartily and sleep soundly. He plays chess. He loves music and enjoys a broad taste, but beats a pulse simpatico with reggae and rap. He is kind, inquisitive; a gentleman with impeccable manners, and a boxer from the old school, with a little late sixties Ali and his own personal now thrown in. Funny. He is a wicked kind of funny.

There are many practical jokes to choose from. My current favorite: Lennox and his friend/ trainer, Scott DeMercado, were once holed up at Len's mom's house in Canada. They were in the parlor, watching the instructive Pamela Lee Anderson/Tommy Lee honeymoon video on cable. Scott was lying on the couch, laid up, ill or injured. Len disappeared and suddenly his mother took his place.

'Len said you wanted to see me, Scott?'
Scott, stuck on the couch, searches frantically for clickers.

'What you watching, honey?'
Clickers are gone.
Hear the wicked snicker off camera.

Lennox 'the Lion' Lewis.

He became the Junior World Boxing Champion one hot day in Santo Domingo. Olympic gold medal winner, South Korea. Undisputed Heavyweight Champion of the World. 'How many fights?' I once asked him. He said, 'Thirty thousand some.' Thirty-nine wins, two losses. He has been knocked out twice. Each time, he came back and, in immediate rematches, knocked his man out. He left Oliver McCall crying, defenseless, his hands hanging at his sides, swaying in the center of the ring. He is the most gracious of losers, but he doesn't like to lose.

He is the third three-time reclaimer of the heavyweight title. It's been a long haul. Lennox chose not to sign on with the reigning boxing promoters and his independence dragged him behind the pack for a long time. He is rarely assessed purely for his consummate skills: some people have craved more 'fight' from him and have left disappointed. Some didn't want to meet him in the ring at all. Mike Tyson was champ in 1992 when he purposely passed the top contender Lennox for man number two. That choice cost Tyson $4 million. Riddick Bowe had to gift Lennox with a belt for passing him over. That charming champion placed the belt in a garbage can during a press conference, apparently for Lennox to retrieve.

Lennox Lewis has taken the sport, the title, back to a world of elegance and sportsmanship – that old-fashioned world that he understands quite well. Respect, mon. It's all about respect. He is a beautiful champion. In 2001, he was nearing the end of his reign. The world was just about to catch up with him.

It is better to have
less thunder in the mouth
and more lightning in the hand.

Interview #1
Holyfield vs Lennox

In October 2000, we're watching the first fight with Evander Holyfield, the one he 'didn't win'.

MM *Does watching this disturb you?*

LL No, no.

MM *You look pretty serious.*

LL I'm very focused right here. In this fight, he was using every kind of trick to pull it out, including pulling my hair. He doesn't know how hard it is to pull it out.

MM *Have you ever gone into a fight with a doubt?*

LL Yes. Well…

MM *When is the last time you had doubt? Did you ever?*

LL I don't have doubt in a normal sense. This is what I have – I don't want to lose. So, if that's a form of doubt, then, the answer is yes and no.

MM *What was that?*

LL I bent down on top of him and he tried to lift me up. It's funny – this fight has many situations. I think this is the fight where he said he was going to knock me out in the third round. For me, I should have gone after him in the third round, because I said to myself, 'No way is he going to knock me out in the third – I'm not going to allow that.' See, that round took a lot out of him.

MM *That was the third round?*

LL Yeah. He shouldn't be disappointed! There's no way he can knock me out in the third round.

See? Those were *glancing* shots, but it caused the crowd to erupt. I was hitting him there with those fast punches. They haven't shown one punch where he's hit me clean. Every one cut through – suddenly, I have cuts above my eye and on my skin. He head-butts. See?

MM *Yeah. Did you think you had won?*

LL Yeah. It was about clean shots. I was so disillusioned with this.

MM *Did you cry?*

LL No. Definitely not. It's funny – I'm still relaxed – taking it all in. I'm saying here that they made some kind of error adding up those scorecards. If I had a promoter who had the advantage – who's taking judges out and paying judges...

MM *Is that your mom coming into the dressing room there?*

LL Yeah. It's funny. Everyone is upset and I'm just there. After the fight everyone's saying, 'Why didn't you knock him out?' and I say, 'Why didn't he knock me out?' You know. Anybody who goes and watches fights can see that I won that. This is where I lost a lot of respect for him, you know? Because he knows he lost it but he still refuses, even to this day he refuses to say that I won. A blind man knows that I won.

MM *A lot of people were talking about that fight.*

LL It elevated me. People were saying I was really a good fighter so they felt sorry for me in one sense. In another sense, some of them said, 'Why didn't you knock him out?' I'm like, 'A knockout is not the name of the game. The name of the game is winning.'

MM *How soon afterwards was your next fight with him?*

LL It was weird the next fight. It's hard training for a fight where you knew you won and now you have to do it again. It's different.

In November 1999, Lennox met Holyfield again. He won, and became Undisputed Heavyweight Champion of the World.

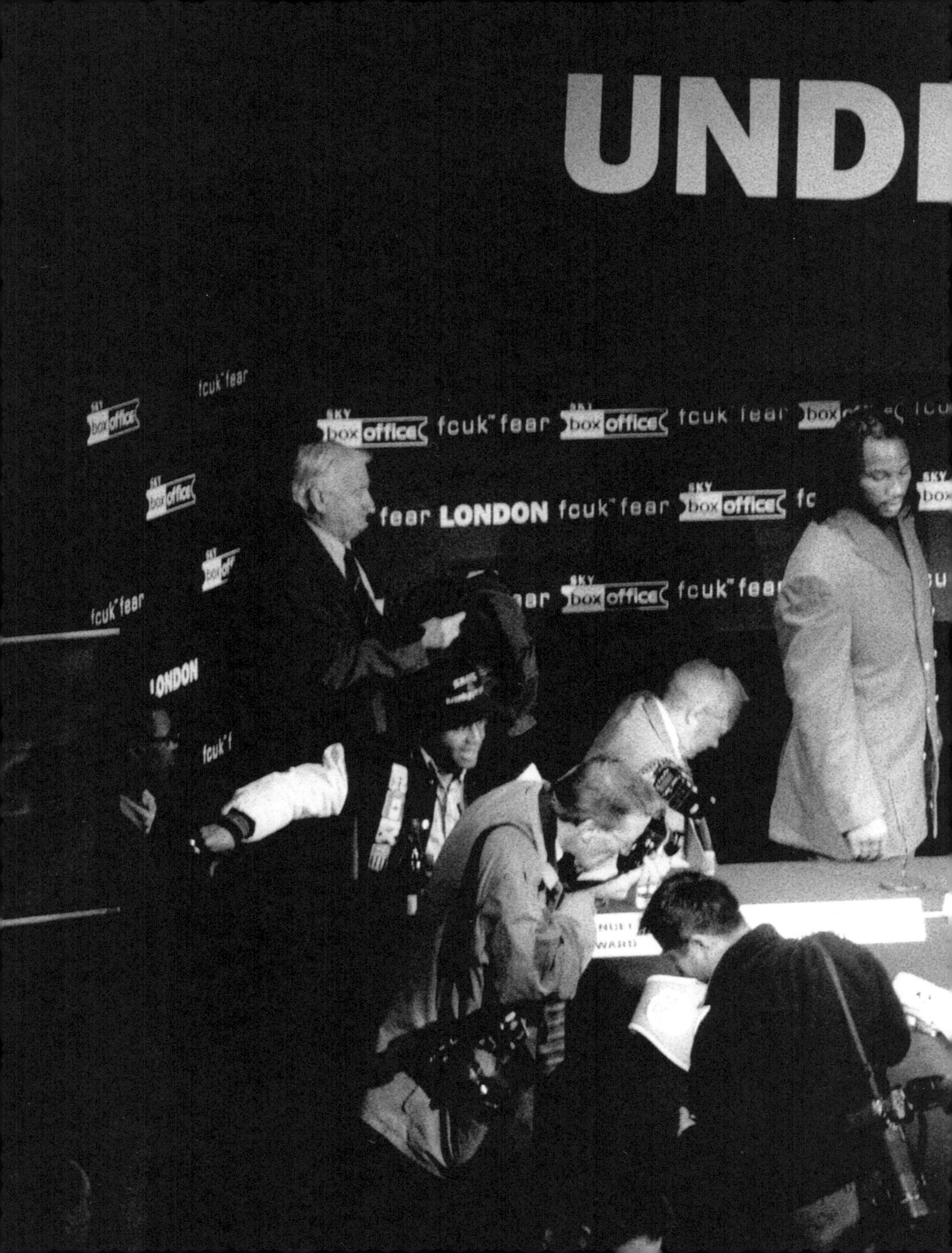
UND
SKY box office
fcuk fear
fear LONDON fcuk fear
LONDON

SPUTED
fcuk fear
SKY box office
fcuk fear
LONDON
fcuk fear
SKY box office
SKY box office
fcuk fear
SKY box office
LONDON

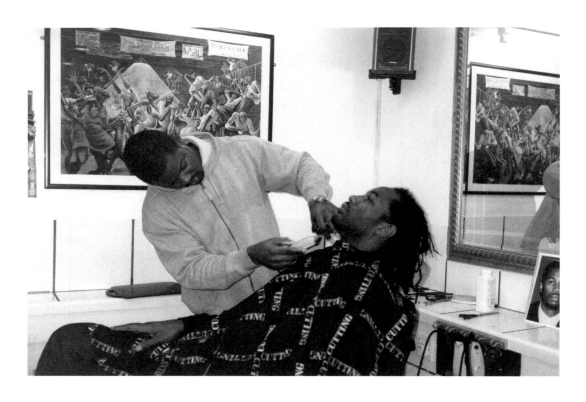

Camp, the Poconos,
early October, 2000

We drove to the Poconos late last night.

The Poconos Mountains, the borsch belt, destination of urban dwellers searching for summer escape. Low hills rising as you leave New York and New Jersey. The Delaware Water Gap – a stunning glacier slice – slips you into Pennsylvania and the highway climbs. We've got woods here, we've got cold. It must be after midnight when we pull into Caesar's Brookdale Resort and the stars are OUT. The crickets are stupendous. Champion crickets, louder and different from any I've ever heard before. Later, Lennox informs me that they are, in fact, birds, not crickets – some crazy-ass insomniac birds.

Either the team or the management has selected for me a Cleopatra, champagne-glass room. Later, as I come to know them, I'd bet *Team* chose it. There is an 8-foot, Plexiglas, champagne bathtub in the living room. I have a round bed. Mirrors above me, mirrors to the left of me, mirrors to the right. I'm a woman with her own troubles. I've driven a rented car to a place I've never seen before with a young man I've just met. At this point I know next to nothing about boxing, yet here I am, alone in the honeymoon suite, the only woman in a training camp full of celibate men. Ironic? You think?

I'd met Lennox a few months back through my friend Lucinda, and asked if I could visit camp and write something about it – I didn't know what. Over sushi, he nodded yes.

'What got you interested in boxing?' I'd asked.

He poked an oyster.

'The trophies.'

Blaise Hart has been photographing Lennox for six years. He has allowed me to supply these words for his beautiful pictures.

Things I learned from Scott on the drive up.

Lennox trains and stays in his room. That's it. He listens to music, watches TV and plays chess. He eats his mom's dinner, maybe a walk afterward. No parties, no booze, no girls. Wednesdays and Sundays off.

He likes science fiction and martial arts movies. He watches a kung fu movie just before each fight. Says he wants to try yoga. He's practicing t'ai chi. A little basketball, a little tennis. 'He's a natural athlete,' says Scott. 'The only true natural athlete I've ever known.'

Lennox has begun to use the word 'pugilist'. It makes him laugh. Later, I show him pictures of Greek athletes boxing, each man tied with leather thongs to a flat slab of rock, an arm's length apart. They'd reach out and whack one another, punch, punch, till one of them died. 'That's grotesque,' says the pugilist.

Lennox lost once, to Oliver McCall. Immediately after the fight, Lennox crossed the ring and asked McCall's trainer to train him. That man was Emanuel 'Manny' Steward. Len had his rematch. McCall quit in the fifth round.

Whoever owns the belts controls boxing. Lennox owns them now. 'Have you heard much about Don King Promotions lately?' asks Scott. 'You haven't. That's because Lennox holds the belts.'

Lennox's focus is imperative. It's a skill. One hundred and ten per cent. Yet, once, while entering the arena, he stopped in his march and gently moved an old woman out of his path and into her seat.

Len is 'Death before Dishonor'. He is all about 'Death before Dishonor'.

There's a team. Seven of them, plus Manny. It's teamwork.

In the gym, Patrick selects the music. It's garage music, underground English techno. The gym is located in the sometime roller rink at Caesar's, obligingly curtained off and freed of its skaters to serve as training central. The ring stands in the center of the room. It's exciting, the ring. It's exciting just to look at it, all red and forbidding, roped off and elevated. Len appears, wearing a red rubber Martian outfit. It's very bumpy. Later, when I know him better, I will not be able to resist just reaching over to touch the bumps on his vest. 'Holds in the muscles,' he explains.

The music fills the room – the very, very hot room. It must be 85 degrees in here. This is one of Lennox's little secrets – he trains in the heat. Sitting on a stool, I ask Scott if he has somehow placed me right in the center of the heat wave. 'It's everywhere,' he apologizes. 'It's hottest in the ring.'

Len straddles a folding chair and chats softly as his hands are wrapped. Manny, and only Manny, wraps him. 'Lennox likes his hands tight.' It's a precise and personal service, and Manny has the touch of a loving nurse. Harold rubs liniment on Lennox's arms and legs. Something like Gatorade, but mauve in color, chills in a bucket of ice – it's some concoction of Joe's. Fresh white towels are piled on a white tablecloth. A Kronk Gym trunk overflows with boxing gloves of all sizes, weights and colors – a cornucopia from Detroit. Ron closes the red velour curtains, shutting out Caesar's autumn frolickers. Patrick turns the music up, this garage music. It's the boys' garage.

Courtney stretches him. For such a big man, Lennox is powerfully flexible. He can turn his shoulders inside out and reach the wall behind him. Courtney and Len chat. Ron and Scott chat. Joe and Patrick chat. Everybody chats here. Later in this eight-week session, when the sparring kicks in and those curtains part again for witnesses, the boys' friends will arrive carrying babies. Boxers and babies – that's a remarkable sight. Now, the exercise begins. What? Jumping jacks? What? Touch your toes? The routine is surprisingly old fashioned. Boys run in figure eights, swinging their arms. Scott wears a T-shirt that reads, 'Refuse to lose'. Bend over, touch the ground, now to the other side – it's follow the leader and that would be Lennox. Now up on the heels and down on the toes. Run in place, slap hands under the thighs, move backwards. Now some coordination movements. Neck rolls, Len's the loosest. What now? Scott goes for wrist twists, so they all do it. Egerton throws in a little hip action. Copy him.

I hear the bell being tested. The three-minute bell. It makes me jittery. Later, I learn what it means to wait for it. Manny tosses a medicine ball. Len tosses it back hard, hitting the ceiling. One of the perforated, dry-board squares pops out of place. Ron climbs a ladder and repairs the damage.

And then, Len leaps into the ring. He LEAPS. He was standing still, and then he was on the ring's edge and climbing through the ropes. He just jumped straight up 4 feet – not a running jump, just a jump straight up. It's impressive. 'That was my judo thing,' he says.

Lennox's shadowboxing will forever remain an image of absolute beauty in my mind. He circles as he punches – north, south, east and west. He is fast and straight and focused. Weaving, backward, little steps, throwing lefts, throwing rights. Howard wipes the sweat away. Eggie shadowboxes on the floor, in front of a mirror. You hear, 'whissph'. It's Lennox, exhaling as he punches. Later in the day, he invites me into the ring and asks me to show him a few yoga postures. I hesitate. Doesn't this access have to be *earned*? I climb in, recognizing an honor when I see one. It's springy in there. And hot. It seems smaller on the inside than it appears from the outside. We do a few easy bends. Courtney shoots me a suspicious, pained glance.

Joe can judge whether Lennox is burning fat or burning muscle. Later that evening we will walk home. Lennox asks me about the Tibetan monk meditators who can stay warm – who can, in fact, dry the dampened sheets wrapped about them while sitting in the freezing temperatures of the Himalayas. I tell him what I know, that the Dalai Lama allowed a doctor to measure it and that the monks were burning muscle; they were in hibernation mode. Len says he heard that they tried to do it in the US; the monks came over and they just couldn't achieve that mode in America.

'Do you think it was something they ate?'

I show him the woodland mint I'd discovered.

'No, mon, it's not mint.'

It's close to 90 now. Lennox moves to the heavy bag.

He dances with that big black bag. He hits, but he parries, he dips, goes under it, lets it brush up against him, moves away from it. The bag is alive, and it wears the face of his opponent, but only he can see it. He moves to the little red bag – the speed bag – and starts doing a mean, whisking, sideways move as he drums out his own personal tattoo. Is there any sound in the world like that little red speed bag? It sounds even better when the champion hits it. It looks so easy. It all looks so easy.

It's a pretty setting, this Poconos palace. A quiet lake stretches out below the boxing gym. During the day, there are playful paddleboats, disguised as swans or dragons or frogs, on the lake. Gum trees and willows and white spruce shimmer in the setting sun. Soon, it will be dark when the boys move into the training gym at 4.00 or 5.00 p.m. The lake outside the wide picture windows will be a black lagoon. They live like monks here for eight weeks. I get the feeling that I'd like to stay.

He's finished. He is weighed and wiped and watered. His shirt is changed, his gloves removed, his shoes untied. He allows the service. What's happening here? It's understood. It's teamwork.

Later that night, we talk. Lennox is wearing a striped cotton sweater, loose pants and a knit cap. Lennox Lewis is one great dresser. Always. He always looks great. Mom has cooked snapper. Courtney is coming in at 11.00 for a rubdown. Len's got piles of business papers, piles of books and piles of movies. No snacks. Low light. Music, of course, but softly now. Lennox plays chess with Scott as we talk. The chess never stops. Often, there are two boards and two games going at once. Often, four, five or six of his monks sit in this quiet maroon suite in the Poconos, silently playing chess. Len usually wins.

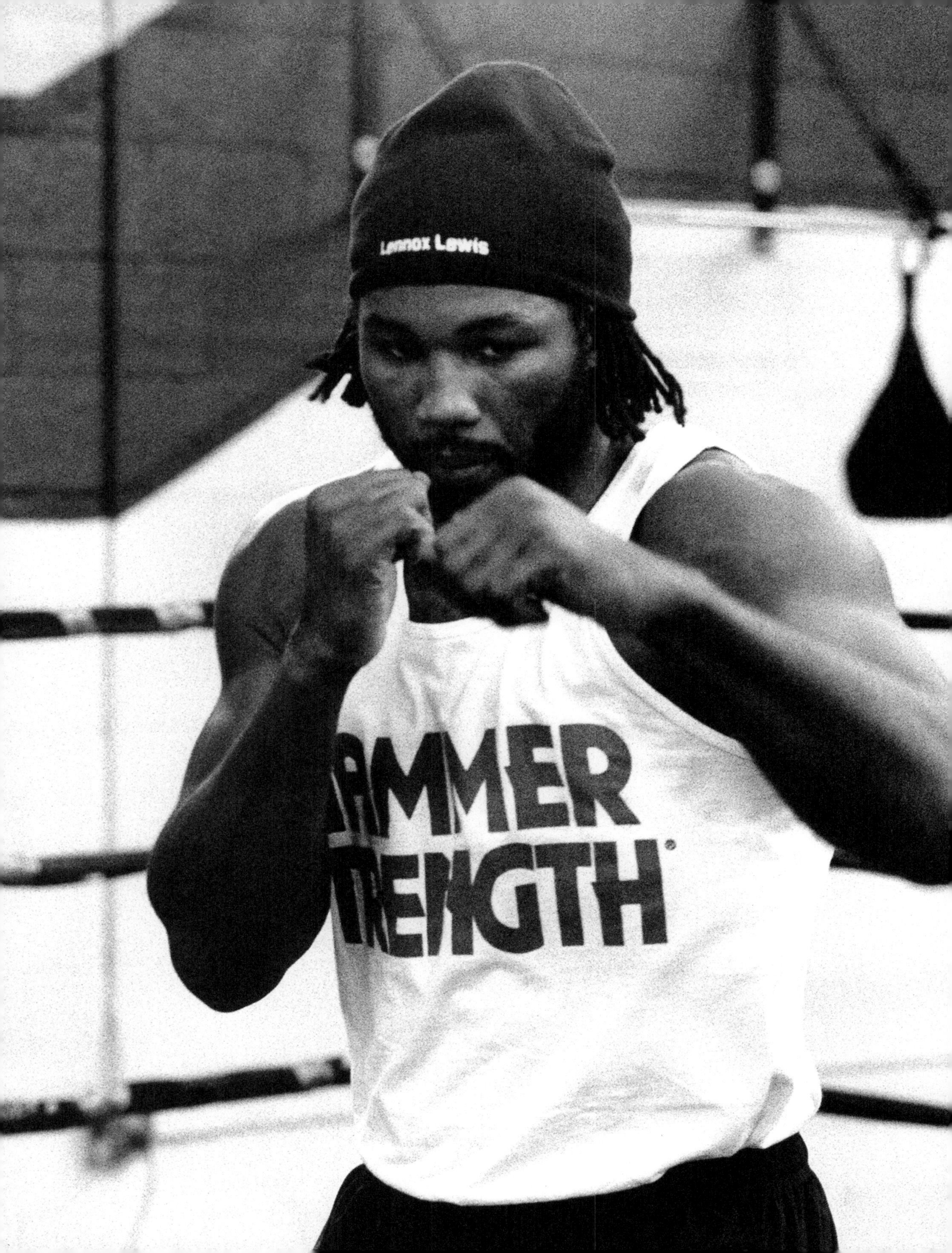
Lennox Lewis

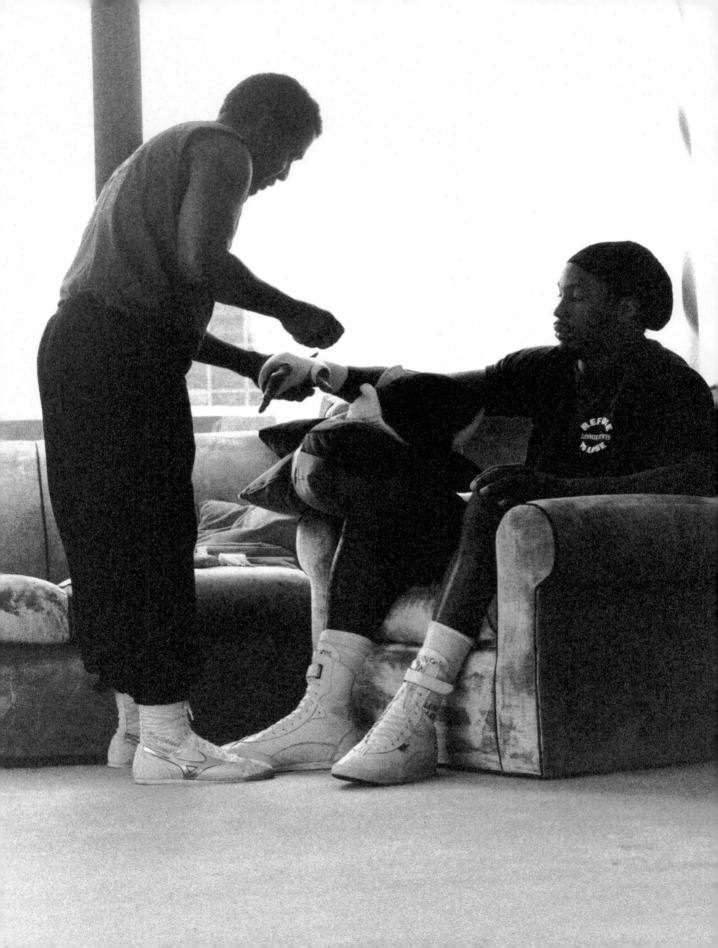

Interview #2 later that night

MM *Have you ever lost a belt or had anyone try to steal it?*

LL No.

MM *Are they better than trophies?*

LL Yeah. Because it's like a graduation. There was a phase in my life where I just got medals. I'd come home and hang up the medals and have a whole wall of medals.

MM *Who is your dream match?*

LL I don't have a dream like that. I wouldn't want to fight Muhammad Ali, because he's the person who got me into boxing. He's an idol – I appreciate what he's accomplished.

MM *Have you been hurt in a fight?*

LL Yeah. It's not a long hurt. It's like [slap] … ahh. But, you have to come back – that's when the discipline comes in. Even though you hit me, I'm not going to show you that I got hurt. I'm going to hold myself, so I don't encourage you. I've been hit really hard and not been hurt. I've had a fighter say to me, 'I don't even know how you got away from that shot in the first round – do you remember it?' And I'm like, 'Did I get hit?' I don't remember it because it's like you're just caught up in the moment and it's all punching. You're such a professional you don't get the full brunt of it – you keep coming back.

It's all about energy. You're blocking it, you're absorbing it and releasing and coming back. It's like you're deflecting the energy this way and bringing it back around. I love the martial arts. I watch kung fu before I step in the ring. It makes me quicker. It makes me feel like a martial artist in the ring. I have that quickness in my mind from seeing it.

The phone rings, Scott answers in a whisper.
    Scott: It's Tanya.
    Lennox: Who? I don't know no Tanya.

MM *Groupies?*

LL I get all kinds. Nutters.

MM *The bell gets to me. When you go back to the corner, and you've got so much to do in one minute, and you're talking to your guys, are they a blur or are they in focus?*

LL I've only had a couple of fights where they've been kind of like a blur. It's because of the excitement around you. You hear the crowd; the referee comes over and says something like, 'Watch your holding.' The cameraman is there. There's a guy right there watching the corner man, making sure he's not slipping you a Mickey or anything. And that's all in a minute. Information, water, everybody's wiping you down, shaking your legs, giving you water. It's like a pit stop. So sometimes it's a blur. Sometimes you listen and sometimes you don't, but these are people that want to help you.

MM *Taking that minute – obviously you usually want it. But is it sometimes awful to stop the round?*

LL Only if you have your opponent hurt and you want to get it over with.

MM *When an opponent says mean things in a clinch, does that ever affect you personally, or does it just roll off you?*

LL I take it all personally. I feel the attitude. I analyze what he's saying. If he's saying something bad about my mother, then, yeah, I take those kinds of things personally. But if he says, 'I'm going to knock you out', if it's just boxing talk, then I don't. Saying evil things, that actually helps me, because I'm going, 'Yeah, alright.' I keep it under control, though. I'm not going to go mad. Control. I don't say anything I don't mean, that's the difference with me.

MM *Do boxers look each other in the eye?*

LL I think you have to, although some boxers don't, they look at your hands. I look at the eyes. You can see then when they're getting ready to throw a punch. It's all focus and determination. I mean my expression changes, it depends on the situation in the fight. I've smiled on many occasions. If I hit you and I know I hurt you, I just smile. It's a mental thing again, that works against my opponent. My personality comes out in a fight. Some people say I show arrogance – I guess so.

MM *Will you know when it's time to quit?*

LL That's the thing about boxing – there's always going to be another guy. It's like King of the Hill. You have to know when to stop. I think about what made Muhammad Ali go on, what made Sugar Ray go on and Holyfield is still going on. I can't answer that question until I reach that point. We've all got our own reasons why we continue. Whether we're in a high position or just want to be in the limelight all the time. You have to stop – if your ego can endure it.

MM *What about in a fight? Would you be able to recognize if you should stop?*

LL That's where the training and the trainer come in. You have to be aware of the mental aspect.

MM *So, you have to count on somebody else to recognize it?*

LL I've never been in that position, and, even if I was, I've reached such a mark in my life that I don't think I would quit just like that. I'd have to have broken ribs.

MM *Can you see when your opponent should stop?*

LL Sometimes. When they're hurt. I'm not thinking about that, though. I'm thinking only about the match. Sometimes a match does turn into a fistfight, then it's just boom, boom, boom. You're taking punches, you're throwing punches – it's too fast a fight. That's not boxing. When it's like that you don't see the moves and the punches and the combinations.

MM *I was surprised today at training to see just how you are cared for by the guys, everything from tying your shoes to wiping you down, wiping the floor underneath you.*

LL It's helping me to be better, the most prime athlete. Everyone knows what to do. For instance, if I'm working on the bag and I'm sweating, I need someone to wipe the sweat away because the sweat is weighing me down.

MM *Literally?*

LL Yeah – because of my shirt. I used to go through three shirts in my workout. And that also helps you stop from getting a cold because if I get a cold then I'm out for like ten days trying to recover. They make sure I'm stretched out, make sure I don't pull a muscle, make sure I don't get dehydrated. My team is watching this. If I make a technical error, people are watching for that. They're also running security. They're watching my energy. Everyone knows what to do and has different jobs. It's great.

MM *So, you are king at the gym. How does all that attention affect you personally?*

LL I am natural with it. They know I'm thankful for it. That's their job. Come back and you're playing chess or tennis, then I don't have that king aspect. I think I got that from my mum. When I was younger and going off to a fight or whatever, she would be all humbling and say like, 'get back in there and fix up your room'. I'd be like 'I'm the best in the world – why do I have to fix up my room?' I always cleaned up my room though.

MM *How do you then expect a girlfriend to treat you?*

LL I think she treats me like a king. On the other hand, I treat her like a princess.

MM *How old were you when you started boxing?*

LL Twelve.

MM *You had not done any boxing?*

LL No. I was living in Canada, going to public school and I was in basketball and football and in track and field at the time. I was like the tough guy in my school. Each school had their tough guys. So, at one of the school dances we challenged this other school's guys to a fight and said, 'Okay, we'll meet at the police boxing program.' My friend and I went every day for two weeks to the Kitchener, Ontario, police boxing club, waiting for these guys who never showed up. A retired police officer, Hook McComb, was running the boxing club. He and my first trainer, Arnie Boehm, they looked at me and said, 'Boy, you know, you should keep it up.' And that's it.

MM *What was the fight about?*

LL Just egos.

MM *Had you been fighting guys when you were angry?*

LL Yeah.

MM *Did you feel like you were on to something?*

LL I liked the aspect it was just you and that other person. You had to be quicker or just smarter than that person, and that was it. That's what I liked about it – that excitement. You could try to knock someone out or just use your brains to stay on top.

Camp, the Poconos,
late October, 2000

I spent my time and drove myself home. I got a call later in the week.

'Hey, you know, after the yoga, well, the champ's hurting.'

'Don't do this to me, Scott.'

'No, really. He wants to know what he should do to counteract it.'

'Don't do this.'

'Courtney's gunning for you.'

It wasn't funny. 'Seriously, it's not funny.'

'Seriously, he's gunning for you.'

It's Wednesday night – 'camp' night. Scott and I are driving across a darkened New Jersey, picking out the hometowns of famous American writers (i.e. William Carlos Williams) from the freeway and sharing free-flowing memories of life-altering experiences.

'Has he ever had a broken heart?' I ask Scott, somewhere outside of Patterson.

Scott laughs. 'Oh, I couldn't say. You have to ask him.'

I've forgotten to do so.

We arrive around 10 p.m. I have a semi-normal room this time: red-flock wallpaper and plastic chrome. I sit outside for a while listening to those 'crickets'.

Breakfast is in the 'Lennox Lewis Training Camp' private dining room. A wooden Hanzel and Gretel point the way, photos of boxing camps past line the *faux* paneled walls. Our men are refueling after the morning run. Most of them wear black or dark blue, velour or stretchy woolens. Lennox sticks his head in to say hello. He is in tight black, head to toe. Surprisingly, he decides to stay – Egerton's omelet looks good.

Patrick dips his silverware in a paper cup full of hot water.

'Do you think that works?' Lennox laughs. 'Why do you do that?'

'We're not the only ones who eat here,' answers Patrick.

Lennox gets his omelet, but it's too big, it hangs off the plate. He's losing his appetite. He thinks he might have flu. He reels off his symptoms.

'I don't like to complain,' he says, and he means it.

'Sounds like flu,' I agree.

Certainly, this would explain the 'hurting'. If he's sick, then it wasn't the yoga.

The waiters are dying to come into the room. Lennox doesn't eat here very often. One young man finally, boldly, comes in and just stands near Lennox, as close as he dares.

'Lennox Lewis. The heavyweight champ?'

'The same.'

'How tall are you?'

'Six foot five.'

'Stand up.' It's an order.

'Later.'

The young man won't leave. He feigns a few punches.

'Don't hurt me,' he says to the champ.

Lennox wouldn't hurt a fly. He has been known to move bugs before someone steps on them.

'Keep the food comin' if you don't want to get hurt, then,' says Lennox.

'Hey, how about that Tyson?' asks the waiter.

'Yeah.'

Lennox asks for some hot water for his tea. The waiter pours him some, leaning in, monopolizing the space so that Lennox will have to move out of *his* way. In a deft move, Lennox moves horizontally – in a seated position – from chair to chair. The waiter's attempt failed. Lennox didn't stand up.

After the water is poured, when the bossy young man steps back, Lennox simply stands for him, all stretchy black arms and legs, looking down on him from up high.

'God,' says the young man.

'Yah, mon.'

This demanding, short, young waiter still cannot leave. There are too many questions; the questions are too personal – weight, height, girth, hair, age – flesh questions. Personal. Somehow insulting. Lennox is never less than gracious. Finally the guy leaves.

'Tough,' I say. 'It's so personal.'

'It always is.'

'Do people treat you as if you're magical?'

He thinks. 'Yes and no.'

'But they want something physical from you. They want your *physicality*.'

'Always. That's why I stay in my room.'

I tell him a story from Norman Mailer's book, *The Fight* – about the young fan following the victorious boxer from the arena, wiping sweat from the champ's body and rubbing it on his own.

Len smiles.

A few weeks later, on press day in the Poconos, I hear him tell a grateful reporter 'in a room full of men, I'd be the last man standing'.

I couldn't have made that up.

Scott tells a Tyson joke he's heard.

'Tyson says, "I went up to the room and the girl gave me her consent." Get it? *Cun*-scent.' I get it first, then Len, then Patrick. I can tell that Patrick and Lennox are embarrassed in front of me.

'What about that Tyson?' I ask.

'Yah, mon,' says Len.

Talk does turn to Tyson. The 'I'll put a bullet in his head' remark Tyson made recently, when asked if he'd be fighting Lennox, is terribly offensive to these guys. Terribly.

'He should be stripped of his license for that remark. It's a threat, isn't it?' asks Ron. 'Truly. That's a death threat.'

'So,' I ask, referring to the latest Tyson fight, 'when you leap over a referee after he has separated you, what should happen?'

'You know, it has to do with the television network. A network has a contract with a fighter. The network hires the commentators. So, the commentators might say like, "It appears Tyson didn't realize that the referee has come between him and so and so." Well, it looks to me and everybody else that's watching that Tyson jumped the ref. He should be disqualified. The commentators might say, "Boy, so and so is trying to break Tyson's arm." Tyson's trying to break so and so's arm, but the commentators say it the way it will look good for Tyson.'

'What about the ear bite. Can you imagine doing something like that? Did he bite off a hunk?'

'He bit it off and spit it out,' Len demonstrates. 'I got to say, though, he was fed up with Holyfield's head-butting. I know how he felt. It would take a whole lot for me to get that mad, but I could. I could get vindictive.'

'Have you ever fought dirty?'

No, they all agree. No.

'Not in the ring anyway,' corrects Egerton, his sparring partner, giving Lennox a raised eyebrow. Egerton has some scars above his deep brows.

'Only just between friends?'

'Yeah,' Eggie answers for him. 'Just between friends.'

'How'd you get that *little* omelet?' asks Len.

'I'm a regular here,' answers Eggie.

Look out, here comes another young waiter. This one informs Lennox that Holyfield has 'lost it'.

'Brain damage,' assesses the young man. 'He was slurring and couldn't think straight. He's damaged.'

Len listens quietly. 'Do you think it could have just been his accent?' asks Len.

'No,' says the boy. 'He's messed up. Doesn't know when to call it quits.'

'Yah, mon,' says the champ. 'A man needs to know when to call it quits.'

'You'll know,' says the boy.

'Yah, mon,' says Len.

Lennox eats spaghetti before a fight. He fights on a half-and-half full stomach. He made spaghetti last night in mom's kitchen. He's using the cookbook, *Cooking for Dummies.* We discuss loosening tomato skins. I admit I like clean-up better than cooking.

'Me, too. I'm great at clean-up.'

Big guffaws from the other side of the table.

'We could have a contest,' I say. 'I'm very good at washing dishes.'

'Me, too,' says Len. 'I love cleaning up a kitchen.'

Oh, Team Lewis laughs and laughs.

Let's introduce the team.

First, of course, is Emanuel Steward, Len's trainer. Manny has trained twenty-nine world champions. He began his career as an electrician. He owns and operates Kronk Gym in Detroit. He's the boss.

Harold 'Shadow' Knight is Manny's assistant trainer. Corner man, fight man. The 'word' man from New Jersey. He keeps the faith.

Patrick Drayton from London. Been with Lennox a dozen years. A runner. Does not suffer fools, etc. Has personally designed some of Len's three-piece suits. He's music. He's the pulse.

Courtney Shand. Known Lennox since they were kids growing up in Canada. Very protective. He is my personal toughest conquest; the yoga didn't help. He's the glue. He keeps it together.

Ron Hepburn, also from Canada. Quiet. Caring. Seems he can do it all. He keeps the calm.

Scott DeMercado. Jamaican. Rode his bike across the USA to impress a girl. She broke up with him when he reached Atlanta. Scott's the bike man, room-mate and chess partner. He's friend, mate, checkmate.

Joe Dunbar is from London. Works with soccer teams. He's the distance. Blood, pulse, weight,

drinks, vitamins, supplements, food – he takes it the distance.

Egerton Marcus. Won a silver the year Lennox won the gold. Canadian. Sparring partner. He knows it. He feels it when Len gets hit. He wears the scars.

Lennox and the guys split – back to their rooms to rest. There's a lot of napping at camp. I stay with Egerton while he finishes that perfect little omelet. Egerton keeps a journal with him. He shows me his poems and then, at my pleading, he sings me a song. It's beautiful. It's heartbreaking. I ask about it. He hesitates, then shares the song's poignant source. He wrote it last Christmas, after his wife gave birth to quadruplet girls. After they died, one by one, in his arms.

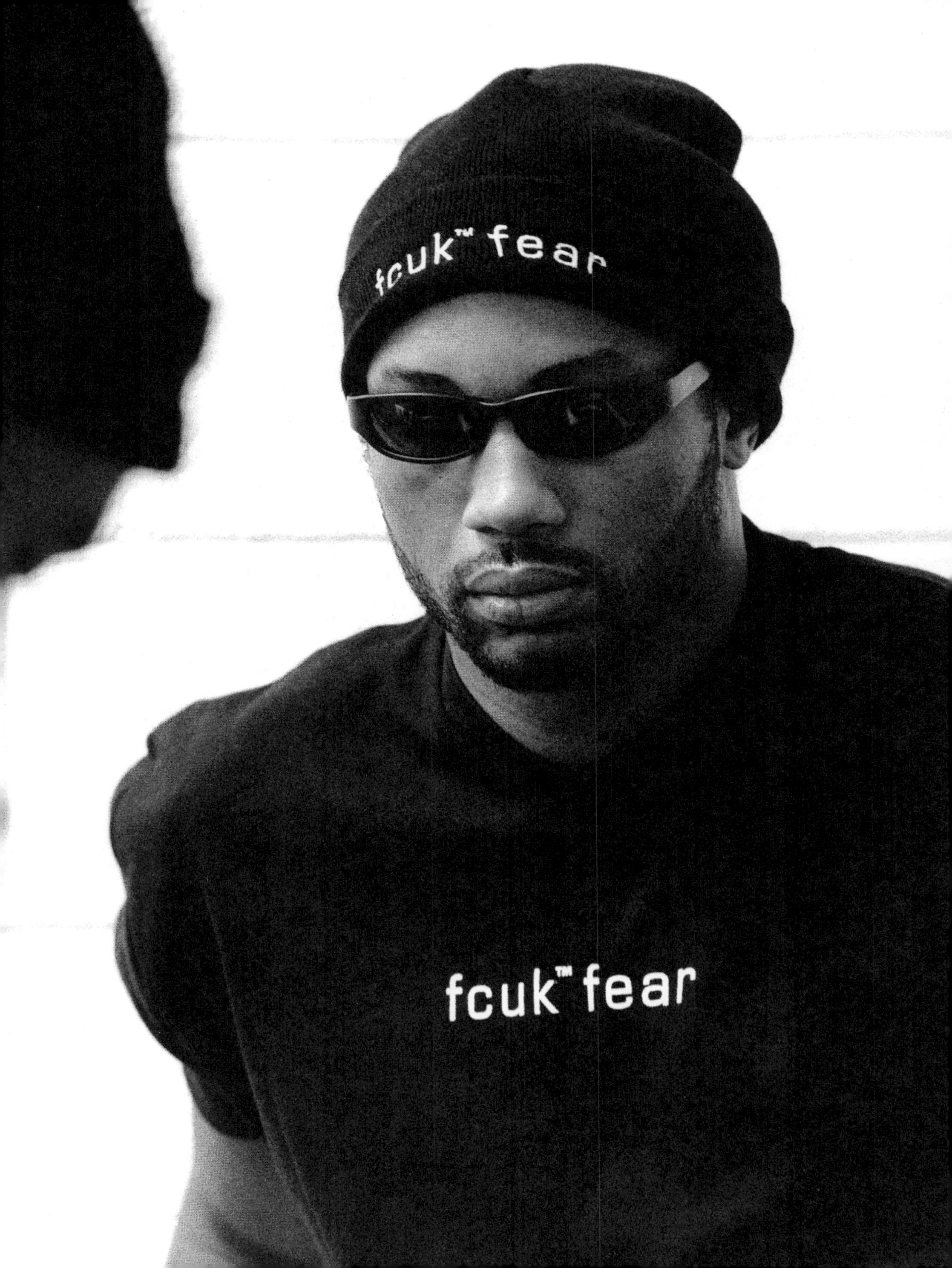
fcuk™ fear
fcuk™ fear

Interview #3 later that night

Turns out Lennox does have flu. No training today, but he can talk.

MM *Joyce Carol Oates wrote a great book called* On Boxing. *One of her notions is that boxers not only mimic anger, that, in fact, their anger is actually ennobled in the ring – 'accommodated' in the ring. Do you agree?*

LL No. Not for me. It's a sport to me. It's me trying to outdo the other person – getting the most points, score the most points. Hit him without him hitting me. It's a game – it's a game of trying to elude. It's a game in which the highly skilled are the ones that are successful. They're using the 'sweet science'.

So, when it comes to anger, you may feel anger in certain situations, but not one hundred per cent of the time, because that just takes away your energy, you know what I mean? You may be angry if you miss a shot, you may be angry if he hits you with a shot but I don't think you're going in there mad. You can go in there mad, yeah, you can go in there mad and pissed off, but it takes up a lot of energy.

MM *How does race play a part?*

LL I think it plays a big part, especially to me as a black boxer. It's hard enough anyway. You don't see too many white heavyweights out there because they can't survive in the game, because there's too many black boxers saying, 'Boy, he ain't gonna win.'

I think for many Americans watching black boxers, they sense the anger. They assume it's racial. You're talking about guys who grew up really poor, a lot of times in the South or in the ghettos, and have suffered their whole lives. Whatever anger they have about their situation in life would've possibly been apparent if they were bus drivers, but since they're in boxing, and because there is that 'mimicry of anger', I think that the audience associates race and anger.

This is not the story in my case. With me it's more about the challenge. It's a one-on-one game and you're saying, 'Boy, I don't want to lose to this person', and if it's a white guy, yeah, it's even more so. You definitely don't want to lose to a white guy, because you realize that for other black boxers out there it's deeper, and you respect that.

MM *Tougher to lose to a white guy. Because the white guy has had advantages in his life that the black boxer didn't have? Or is it that you think the white guy's weaker, physically, and you don't want to lose to a weaker opponent?*

LL I think it's the one more advantage thing, maybe. I don't think it matters who's weaker or whatever. I think it's the fact that we've been oppressed, and if you lose, you're being oppressed even more, because it's like a person stole your power.

MM *Are you able to get a sense of how others see you?*

LL I intimidate a lot of people. I wonder why. I think it's my presence. Maybe, they don't realize that I create that aura. They probably feel uneasy about it because they don't know what's going to happen. I do. I can visualize the future. I use visualization as a part of my preparation. I think it's very necessary for all athletes to do that. It's like a baseball player who can actually see the pitch before he throws it. So, they've already seen the pitch and they know what to do automatically.

MM *So, what's the truth behind no sex before a fight? Sperm-retention syndrome?*

LL I don't agree with all that. From my standpoint as a boxer, mentally, you have to be very focused. Sure, the aspect of looking forward to being with your woman afterwards gives you strength. I agree with not thinking about your woman, having that little edge, otherwise it can take your energy away. Having an orgasm is like running up the stairs. That's as much energy as you use up. I think three weeks before the fight is a fair time to kind of just cut it out. You focus and feel a lot better. You're stepping into the ring without all these things bothering you, without all these things on your mind. Being in the game so long, I realize what doesn't have to bother me. My main focus is on what's in front of me.

MM *What does it take to be the Heavyweight Champion of the World?*

LL Determination, willpower, and vision, a little bit of luck, perseverance, patience, desire, guts and will.

MM *Does playing chess help you box?*

LL Yes, because there's a strategy involved in playing chess, and there's a strategy involved in stepping into the ring because each opponent is different and you have to work out a strategy to beat them. It helps you focus as well, and it helps in decision-making, whether to throw a right hand or a left hook or to move, just like how in chess you would capture an opponent's pawn with a knight or bishop – but which one do you actually do? So you have to make the right decisions.

MM *Do you see several moves ahead in the ring?*

LL Yes. Absolutely. Move a man into the corner, all of a sudden when he reaches that corner, you know exactly what you're going to do to him. You try and trap him into that. Like a spider to a fly.

MM *Here's my daughter's question: 'How can you take it when you get hit in the face?'*

LL You build up a resistance. When I first started boxing and I got hit in the face, I hated it. Actually I got hit on the nose and it made my eyes water and I hated it. After a while you learn that defense is very important in boxing. You learn how to not take the full brunt of a punch and you learn to move with it and not be in that position where you're going to get the full brunt of it.

MM *I read that often Ali would concentrate less on building his own speed and more on taking punches. I also read that he would assimilate the pain by moving it from the place hit to another, less vulnerable place in his body. Does that sound right?*

LL I can see in one aspect how that can work, but as far as if you get hit in the shoulder and bring the pain out through the hand, I don't think you can do that. What you have to do is more of a relaxed thing; you just get hit and forget that you got hit there. Wave it off. You've told your mind that it's not going to affect you. So, you absorb it and spread it throughout your whole self so you're not feeling the whole shock of it. Go with it, move with it.

MM *Does your skin build up a resistance?*

LL Yeah.

MM *More daughter questions?*

LL Yah, mon.

MM *'Do you wear an apron when you cook?'*

LL If I'm cooking and it gets messy I'll wear one. I will. I won't wear it if my friends are around.

MM *'What's your favorite animal?'*

LL Lion. And the main reason is because it's the king of the jungle.

MM *They don't really live in the jungle, the king of the beasts.*

LL I've always wondered what would happen if you put a tiger and a lion together.

MM *I assume the Romans tried that.*

LL But which animal won?

MM *I don't know. On any given day...*

LL But the lion has a mane, so you can't really get to its skull.

MM *'Tell me a joke.'*

LL I don't have any. And you know why I don't have one? Because I've got friends that are always telling me jokes, dirty jokes or jokes that don't make sense. Long-winded ones.

MM *'What's your least favorite part of your body?'*

LL I guess my face.

MM *What would you like people to know about you or recognize in you?*

LL That's a difficult question. What would they *want* to know about me? What do I feel they *ought* to know? I don't want to give them everything.

MM *Do you think people generally* get *you?*

LL Some do. A lot of people identify with my lifestyle. 'He's a nice guy.' I represent a certain type of people. I'm not saying like Tyson is darkness and I'm light, there's just different aspects. You have Holyfield fans out there who are Christian, and go more for him because he's that way, and not for me because I don't say what I am or who I pray to. There's always a good and evil side if you're going to put two men against each other. Whether it's for money or honor. There's that constant battle.

MM *Do you ever sneak a girl into camp? That's my question.*

LL No.

MM *Would you tell me if you had?*

LL At this point, yes.

MM *Do you get nervous?*

LL Not anymore. Amateurs get nervous.

MM *What do you represent as champion?*

LL Boxing is looked at as a rough sport. Yet, I don't make it seem that way, I make it seem like a true sport, not just primal or animalistic. I kind of glorify it. I'm a gentleman fighter. I'm a better edge on a rough edge.

MM *Why do you think that we invest such emotion in the heavyweight champions? Why fighters?*

LL Because we're gallant.

MM *Joyce Carol Oates also writes that a fight is like a dance.*

LL It's only a dance if you're winning.

Interview #4   Emanuel Steward

MM *What don't people understand about Lennox?*

ES To begin with they don't really know what his nationality is. Born in England, Jamaican parents. Raised in Canada. Boxing for Britain, gold medal for Canada. A lot of the time now, he's in America. So that's why you see on my jacket that I have four different flags: the Canadian, the American, the Jamaican and the British. He's a world champion, and it really bothers me sometimes that people don't see that. He belongs to the world. That right there is one thing.

Many people would like him to be open about his private life all the time and have girls hanging all over him. He's one of the most desirable and sought-after men that I've been involved with in my career and he doesn't appear an excessive womanizer. The fact is that Lennox has a beautiful girl, but he doesn't flaunt her. He doesn't try to pass it off with her all over him or after a fight hugging and kissing him. That's the way that he is. He thinks it would be very embarrassing for them to do that.

MM *He told me he didn't like girls having their picture taken with him because maybe they haven't told their father that they're dating him yet.*

ES One of the things women like about Lennox is not only is he a handsome guy, but he's a perfect gentleman. Very polite. And they're attracted to that. I think the fact that he doesn't put much importance on accepting all the media requests is crucial. Being a world champion and not being in scandals and things and being respectful of people – these are the most important things to him. He's very strong in his convictions and he's got a lot of principles, which is, I would say, one of the most impressive facts about him, and he's willing to sacrifice for it.

MM *Explain boxing to me.*

ES First of all, boxing is the most basic sport. It's strange and barbaric and the basic nature of it is to enclose two guys and they have to use their physical body to try to hit and destroy each other. That's what the nature of boxing is. Before we had anything else, we had boxing. It has a solemn dramatic element. You feel the danger and balance and you can't get away from it. People can say what they want, but that's an element that a lot of people like. Then, throughout the ages, it picked up the skills.

There was a guy named Gentleman Jim Corbett, and this other guy named John L. Sullivan, one of the old tough guys – the big moustache, the guy that used to drink the liquor and could look a guy in the heart. So then, here comes this San Francisco banker – suit and tie, bow tie, type of guy. Sullivan gets in the ring and he's destroyed by a guy dancing around him, hitting him and not letting him hit back, putting movement and rhythm and motion in it. People discovered it, and called it the beauty of boxing.

Then you had the Muhammad Alis – a mixture of two individuals in there – physically strong but also skillful, very tough and durable inside. Boxing requires a tremendous amount of intelligence. It's not just about the physical element, not just who can lift more to be the Heavyweight Champion of the World. Who is the tallest, who jumps the furthest, who is the biggest, who weighs the most? You can't do that. It's the individual inside. That's more important than the physical attributes.

When you find a guy like a Lennox Lewis who has physical strength and develops a tremendous amount of natural skills and techniques – this is a very tough, tough individual. That's who will become a great fighter. To watch a guy move around and punch and move back and in and out and outsmart his opponent as well as beat him with physical strength and skill … say what they may about boxing, it's still probably the most exciting thing between two athletes going against each other. When you have a truly world class boxing match, encompassing the world, and those two guys are in an enclosed area and the entire world is watching – there's no element in any Super Bowl game that is like the individuals in this.

MM *What is unique about Lennox?*

ES Lennox combines so many beautiful qualities of a boxer. Most boxers are very physical, such as a Tua or a Mike Tyson. Some guys are very skillful, like a Muhammad Ali, but he didn't have much physical strength. Lennox combines all of that, including intelligence; he's extremely intelligent and very analytical. In addition, he has tremendous punching power. To me he's the epitome of a boxing champion, and an intelligent person, inside and outside of the ring. I've trained many boxers and Hall of Famers. Lennox, he's the complete package.

MM *Do you think the great boxers are peaceful?*

ES I think so. Well, a lot of guys think it's about being tough, being arrogant, being as bad as you can, and that's just not it. You have to look at history and see what prevails – it's a generational thing. That's probably why we're more accepting of a violent boxer right now. Lennox is a good thing for boxing, the guy who is totally polite.

MM *Is that one of the problems for Lennox? Do people want him to be bad?*

ES What has happened is that even when he's boxing, outside the ring is one thing, but even in the ring, Lennox is too much of a gentleman. And that's when I say to him, 'We have to become a little bit more aggressive in the ring.' If you're going to box and play it like a chess

game, it's not going to work. You have to be intelligent about it, but you have to come in and be more explosive. He's beginning to change. He's showing so much more personality. In and outside of the ring. He has tremendous confidence in himself. And he brings a lot of pride to the sport. When he's in training he's a very quiet, reclusive-type person, but he's very warm.

MM *Does he train with more discipline than other boxers?*

ES He and Tommy Hearns.

MM *I read that Rocky Marciano wouldn't allow people to say his opponent's name. Superstitions?*

ES Lennox is not like that. He's not superstitious. Very, very open about that. He's got more undefeated titles than any champion in history. Just look at his record. The thing that attracts me to him is that I always know exactly where he's coming from. That's the certain quality in a person's character that I always like. I enjoy being with him and I am refreshed by him and his team's young generation. I look forward to camp.

MM *What fights would you rewatch?*

ES Oh, Ali fights, one or two of those. Frazier. The character of certain individuals that made them a star was that they were so strong inside. With Muhammad Ali and Frazier it was not so much the technical skills of either one; it was the fierce determination. One guy would have a good round and then the next round would go the other way. It's what's deep down inside. That's what makes great athletes. I've been with Lennox in a couple of fights where I've seen him have that tremendous amount of strength. On the surface, he's such a calm person that it's misleading. That let me see the internal toughness. You can't give that to a guy – he has to trust in himself.

MM *How would you describe your job? When do you know you've brought the fighter to his pinnacle? How do you know he's ready?*

ES First of all you have to understand the make-up and the personality of the individual. And then you have to get inside of his personality, how he thinks and functions. I know how Lennox thinks. He likes to surprise people. I know the nature of him now. He hates for others to know what he's doing. So you understand that kind of privacy. Even in the ring you understand how he thinks. He goes through the whole thing the night before. He's right up above me; I can hear him thinking, almost! I'll go knock on the door, because I know how he is.

In his case, you're trying to hone and develop his skills and to get him in shape. You get him in shape gradually. Lennox is such a perfectionist; he wants to do everything right away. You got to do it gradually. Slow him down so he peaks at the right moment. At that moment, the best of everything, he feels good physically and emotionally. I have to get a gauge and understand him and study his body and study his mind, so we don't get there too soon. So he's right there. In any sport, you can say, well I played tennis yesterday and was perfect, and the next day you say, I did everything right, I don't know what's wrong with me today. I cannot afford that in my business. We don't have the luxury of having a team and doing a season. If you lose, you are no longer champion of the world. You lost the crown.

I have to bring him up to that peak. I have to control what goes into his body, what goes into his mind. And then, make sure that he's realistic about what's going to happen. The night before a fight, I talk to Lennox about what's going to be the scene. He gets it. And I don't think anyone in boxing does that better.

MM *When he's in the ring and the fight is happening, can you control anything then?*

ES No, I just make adjustments on what I see is taking place. In the main training camp, I make sure he's training properly. He doesn't overtrain, he doesn't undertrain. When he gets near, I'm going to slow him down so we can hit that peak of performance. So, I do that, and during the fight I see sometimes there's a chemistry that will take place between two boxers that you can't anticipate. A certain style, or the fans are a little crazy, or whatever. So, I have to wait until I see the chemistry and then make an adjustment. If I think he can get him with a left hook, we'll change the training. That's why you have to have that experience, so that you can make quick judgments right away. You have about forty-five seconds, that's all. You don't have time-out periods. You got ten or fifteen seconds to get back to performance. Clean him and give him some water and refresh him, put some Vaseline on his face and make a quick adjustment and if you're talking too long and the bell rings – it's over with. You're disqualified.

MM *Disqualified? He's got to be up?*

ES Up and moving when the bell rings. It's a pressure business.

MM *I know Lennox achieves almost a trance-like concentration. Do you do the same thing?*

ES Yes. I don't see anyone or hear anyone around me. It all comes down to me being the head guy that can make quick decisions that can alter this man's entire career. It's much different than in other sports. You get so emotionally attached. In Lennox's case particularly, he's such a wonderful, caring person and you really care about him beyond just an athlete. We've become more like a family. So it's not someone I'm just working with. It would hurt me to see him lose.

MM *Do you ever get mad?*

ES Not really. I just make him pick it up. Lennox responds to it. We were at a fight in Ireland and I said, 'Lennox, it's time to close the show. Let's get this guy out of here.' Before the next closing bell rang, Lennox had thrown three right uppercuts and just walked away. I mean he responds. He never says anything, but he responds.

MM *I've been watching his fights with him, and as he explains it, I can begin to see him trying to get the guy in the right position. Is that what all fighters do?*

ES Not all. Lennox is very intelligent. He'll throw certain punches and wait and watch to see which way you move, whether you block him with your hand or maybe you like to duck, and he'll do it and step back and act like he's going to take an extra step and then catch you. Either he sees you're going to duck down, and he'll act like he's jabbing, but he'll come in bam, bam, bam. He's very intelligent. A lot of his quick knockouts are not just coming from strong punching, but because he's just so quick to analyze his opponents right away.

MM *I asked him about his quick knockouts, asking if he feels he should linger a little, make the fight last longer and he said, 'I don't get paid for overtime.'*

ES And it's funny, when the fight is over, he'll come up to my suite and stop by. I'll have some Crystal and he'll say, 'It's so nice to be up here drinking champagne instead of down there fighting. It's much better.'

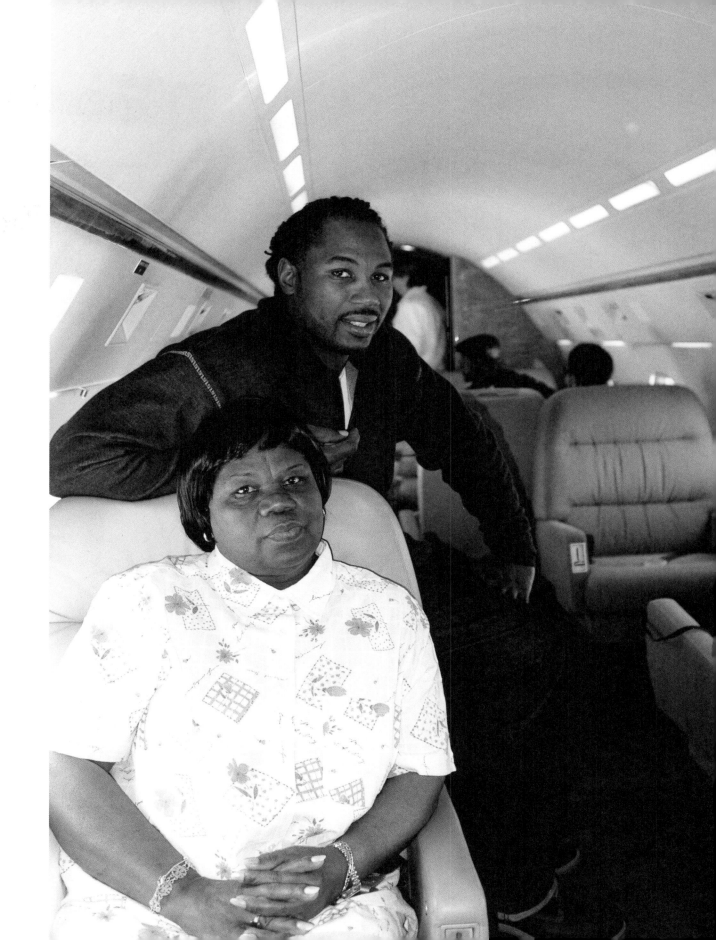

Las Vegas
April, 2001

Lennox trained for the Rahman fight in Las Vegas. He stayed in a two-story, white stucco house, adjacent to a golf course. He had air conditioning and shag carpet. A big TV and a kitchen. Mom was down the road, still cooking his dinners. Prince was in town, the wonderful Prince Poku, from Ghana – Lennox's business associate and fellow conscience. Another good man. Lennox knows that it's crucial to have good people around him. That's why mom is here. Nobody's more good people than Violet Lewis.

Lennox is going to play a cameo in Steven Soderbergh's *Ocean's Eleven*. He's been hired to portray the Heavyweight Champion of the World in a fictional title fight. The filming of Len's part has been postponed for a week, even longer. It's a bad idea, this postponement. Lennox needs to get to South Africa.

Camp is a bit tense. There's no common ground here as there was in the Poconos. Everybody drives. If you looked down on Las Vegas from the moon – and I've been assured you can see its neon splendor from there – you'd find gridlock incongruously balled up in the middle of the open desert. Our boys are right in the middle of it. They drive to the gym; they drive to each other's rented houses. They're often late. They drive from here to there, and that unity, so thoroughly palpable in the Poconos, has suffered. Not evaporated. But suffered. Lennox and Scott are fighting. Bickering. Fighting, actually – headlocks and choking. Scott says he wants to bite him right here, the fleshy part, under the arm. Lennox says he can't really hit Scott, wouldn't want to harm his knuckles on his friend's nose. It's frustration setting in – camp fever mixed with a wanton dose of testosterone and some good old King of the Hill. Lennox is a little heavy. He's older. He's thirty-five now. He's a big man. It's hard for big men to take the weight off.

My tape recorder keeps going out. I scribble notes like: 'A gypsy fortune teller once read his

palm (before the Olympics). She told him that he'd have two kids, he should stay away from the color green, that a black cat is lucky and that he would be rich and special.' And, 'He hasn't cried since he was a kid.' He'll enjoy not being famous. 'I'll get away with a lot more.' He loves to answer 'yes and no'. His favorite answer. It's become a joke, really. I can answer for him now.

He tells me it's not time for him to quit yet.

'Would you retire and come back?'

'Yes and no.'

'Believe in destiny?'

'Yes. And no. I saw something written one time. It said, "There are many different doors you can choose from. When you get to the end of a path, that's your destiny." '

I suggest he should wear shorter shorts in the ring. Really, those homeboy baggies are yucky. Look at the pictures of Ali and Liston, everybody. Sugar Ray. They showed some leg! They looked great.

No answer.

'Are you in touch with your feminine side? Yes and no?'

Yes. He will ask for directions when lost. He gets his hair done by women. He wears Secret deodorant (women can tell by smelling him, he says). He uses body lotion on that velvety skin.

'Lennox, do women want to sleep with you because you're the Heavyweight Champion of the World?'

'No, mon. They *like* me.'

We're in fake pre-fight mode. Lennox and the team are in a trailer, parked behind the MGM Grand Hotel, waiting. It's a movie, mon. You wait. We're drinking Jolts to stay awake. Blaise is trying to figure out how to get a picture of Julia Roberts kissing Lennox. He could ask? No. There's some talk about South Africa, not much. Lennox is anxious to be on his way to Johannesburg. A couple of those long-winded jokes are thrown into the stale air and dissected. Blaise asks Lennox where in town he got his mandatory hepatitis shot.

'In the arm, mon.'

Prince Naseem, the British featherweight champion, stops by. Shoptalk. It's nice hanging with these guys. We know each other now. Even Curtney accepts me now. It's really 'Courtney', but wardrobe spelled his name wrong on the white satin shirt they had made up for tonight's fight scene. *Curtney*. I assure him it will never read.

Ten minutes.

Len is up. And you know what he does? He does it all! He does his warm-up. He stretches, he shadowboxes, he hits the mitts with Manny. He gets a sweat up. He dresses. Harold greases him down. They do everything. Patrick even puts on the music. They do everything, and I get to watch. I get to be in the dressing room because it's fake! But the tension in the room, the ingrained anticipation? It's real. Courtney takes my hand and puts it on Len's arm.

'Feel this.'

'It's hard.'

I've felt Lennox's arm before. His skin is soft, the texture is cushy. But, at this moment, he is hard as a rock. The hypodermic needle would shatter.

'Why does that happen? Fight or flight?'

'Adrenaline? Maybe,' says Courtney.

It happens immediately before every fight. It's happening tonight, before shooting a movie in Las Vegas.

'Pavlovian,' I say.

'Pavlovian?' repeats Lennox, who, as we know, misses NOTHING. 'Definition.'

I explain the Russian, his dogs, the food, the bells.

'Yah, mon, that's me, just a Pavlovian dog.'

The Pavlovian Pugilist.

'Lennox,' I ask, 'do you know what makes you hard?'

Oh, Team Lewis laughs and laughs.

Later that night, Lennox will stand in the ring at the MGM Grand for hours. He won't sit, he won't leave the arena as the movie crew flutters about, shooting close-ups, shooting crowd shots. Blaise caught him the one time he sat down, looking serenely poised and relaxed. Blaise thinks it's funny, this shot of Lennox in the ring with the lights on, the opponent in his corner, the paid crowd of extras cheering, and Lennox is sitting in his corner with his arms spread across the ropes. With his legs crossed. Later, I ask Lennox why he didn't go back to the trailer, why he wouldn't sit. He didn't even take a sip of water!

Easy. Vladimir Klitschko was in the ring. Klitschko is a contender; Lennox might fight him at some future date. Vladimir sat down. Vladimir drank water. He even ate something. Klitschko left the ring for a few minutes. Lennox stayed. Lennox stood. Lennox was psyching the Ukrainian OUT. Pavlovian? That *sweet science*? It never stops working.

Around three in the morning, Lennox is wrapped. We climb in the car, Len in the front seat. Scott's pulling out of the parking lot when, whoops! ... Here comes Julia. She leans in the window and plants a wet one right on Lennox as Blaise scrambles for his camera. Too late. She's gone.

'Oh, those luscious lips,' says Lennox, sighing. The champion turns and looks over his shoulder at Blaise. He laughs and laughs. Blaise snaps him from waist level.

Nelson Mandela and Walter Sisulu in the prison yard, 1966.

Johannesburg
April, 2001

Jim Lampley of HBO (Lennox's network) interviewed Lennox in his dressing room in Johannesburg shortly before the fight with Rahman. The two men enjoy this give and take; they have a nice rapport. However, the next time Lennox faced Rahman, he chose not to do pre-fight press.

Q *Lennox? We're ready when you are. You ready?*

A Yes. I'm coming.

Q *So you obviously would agree with the notion that you're better now than you've ever been before?*

A Yes.

Q *And obviously we would all agree that you're better technically now than you've ever been before.*

A Yes.

Q *Are you better conditioned now than you've ever been before?*

A Yes.

Q *Is that because you work harder, Lennox, or is that because all the years of training and knowledge give you a better understanding of how to harness everything?*

A Yes. And I don't waste a lot of energy.

Q *In Rahman, do you see a guy who can do more than one or two things?*

A Yes. Absolutely.

Q *So what are his strengths?*

A Right-hand jab. And he's defensively good.

Q *More dangerous than Tua?*

A No. Well, yes. Tua has this great left hook that he really counted on.

Q *The heart of the whole matter, it seems to me at this point, based on what everybody's writing and how everybody sees this, is are you taking this fight light?*

A They say that every time.

Q *The definition of that comes from one question. If you were fighting Mike Tyson in Johannesburg?*

A I'd be here earlier.

Q *If you were fighting Vladimir Klitschko?*

A Earlier.

Q *Rahman: do you have any personal conversations with him? Do you know him at all?*

A Seems like an alright fellow.

Q *That's as far as it goes? So you don't know him beyond the totally superficial?*

A Right. I'll probably invite him to my party after.

Q *Did you invite Botha to your party after?*

A Yes, I did.

Q *Did you invite Tua to your party after?*

A No.

Q *Has anybody come? Of the opponents that you've beaten? Has anyone shown up at your post-fight party?*

A Botha came to one of my parties but it wasn't after a fight.

Q *How impatient are you getting for the fight that everyone thinks would define your career?*

A Not impatient at all.

Q *So you feel less urgency about it than say six or eight months ago?*

A Yeah. I mean, he knows where I'm at. If he wants to fight. I'm not chasing him. He needs to chase me.

Q *Are you more and more convinced that Mike doesn't really want the fight?*

A Yeah. As time goes on. I'm not pondering and sitting near the phone or anything like that. I'm not really worried about it.

Q *You're relatively untouched, aren't you?*

A If I was always definitely taking a lot of punishment in these fights, I would probably retire.

Q *Do you worry about what people are going to say ten years from now? How you rank? How great you were, etcetera?*

A No, I don't. Not really. It doesn't really cross my mind. That question has always been asked of me, but I just basically fall where I may fall. Doing the best job I could've done, and am doing.

Jim's finished, but there's one more question from the peanut gallery.

Q *I have a question, Lennox, about the weight – the unofficial weight of two sixty-eight. What are you going to officially weigh? Stripped down.*

A Two fifty-six maybe.

Q *But how many rocks, lead weights and stuff – you're playing with us, right? You enjoy the fact that people think you're overweight. And you're playing with us, right?*

The Dressing Room

We caravan to Venus.

We ride in white cars, Mercedes and BMWs, driven by white mercenaries, Australian and British, who share horror stories from Rwanda and high-speed driving techniques picked up at anti-hijacking seminars. For security reasons, we never take the same route twice, but unfortunately, for us, all roads lead to Carnival City – the outskirts of Johannesburg. Tonight's event: Lewis vs Rahman.

Carnival City is a circus of tent tops by day, a nightmare of neon by night. It's too small; five thousand seats under the big top. Not a bad seat in the house, they say. Seen from a mile away, across a dry South African plain, it looks like a truck-stop whorehouse on Venus. When I saw it for the first time, when I first followed our boxer into the underground bowels of this coliseum, I thought, 'It's going to be a cockfight.' Slated for April 21 in America, it's now April 22 in Africa. They're fighting at five o'clock in the morning.

Lennox correctly weighed in at 253 pounds, only 3 pounds over his last weight for the Tua fight in November 2000. Later there would be charges that he was grossly overweight. The controversy began even before the weigh in, when Lennox obligingly stepped on a scale, dressed head to toe in heavy, hip hop wear, work boots and all. Two hundred and seventy pounds of smiling champion, bored with the flesh-ritual, trying to play with it, shake it up. 'Heavy' stuck to him like tar and feathers. So later they'd say he was disrespectfully heavy, forgetting that the rumor began when he was fully dressed. And playing with them.

It's still dark, that cold dark before dawn. It's 3.30 a.m. when we arrive. Lights had come on back at the Kaponong Hotel compound around 1.30. Time had been screwy here for many days; heavy training at 3.00 in the morning, following a run at 2.00. Sleeping by day. Trying to.

We climb out of our luxury vehicles, slam those German doors and Team Lewis walks swiftly and with purpose through back circus corridors. I feel so excited. Nervous or excited? The talk show psychologist's question. Not nervous. Yes, excited. Many hours later, I would ask Len, 'Did you have a premonition?'

'Yes,' he would reply.

'What was it?'

'It's too private.'

Later still, I learned that he'd been losing at chess all week. Lennox never loses before a fight. During the stormy afternoon following the fight, Scott revealed that he had dreamed of the knockout while in Vegas. In the dream he saw Len go down, exactly as he would go down. And, did you tell him? It was a rhetorical question.

I slide into the dressing room, buffered for inconspicuousness between men with a mission. I had never asked for permission to enter – Blaise did that for me. One night during training in Las Vegas, as Scott chopped vegetables, Blaise asked Lennox if Melissa could come into the dressing room. Blaise said he saw Scott's knife stop, poised in midair. Scott didn't look up. Women are not, as a rule, *welcome* in a boxer's dressing room. Len said, 'I'll let you know.' Scott smiled and went back to his chopping.

I'd been invited into the dressing room *after* the Tua fight: 'when the fight is over, get down the corridor ahead of him, stand at the door, wait'. I did just that, taking hold of one leg of the corner man's blue stool and surfing his wake through the crowd. Len thundered down the hall, spotted me and nodded me in. That night, after he beat Tua in a decision, the belts stayed at home and the music went on. It went UP. It was blasting, and there was Lennox, after twelve rounds with the pugnacious little Samoan, there was Len, dancing. Dancing in his blood-spotted shorts. In his sweat and Vaseline and sewn up dreads. Dancing with his gloves on. He danced for fifteen minutes. All the guys danced. The doctor came in for urine and waited, smiling, tapping his toe. The Heavyweight Champion of the World was dancing now. He could pee later. Then, Len stopped dancing, and as Courtney threw the belts into a duffel bag, and Frank changed out of his Union Jack suit, and Harold gathered up the paraphernalia of the fight, Lennox became perfectly, completely still. Life moved on around him as the music continued to play, but the champion stood still. His eyes were closed. He 'absorbed'.

Months later in New York, on the road from Las Vegas to South Africa, while he relaxed in an armchair and allowed children to bury him in stuffed animals, Blaise said, 'We have a question', and Lennox answered, simply, without waiting for the question, 'Yes'. I was unaware that Blaise had just asked this groundbreaking favor of the man – this 'woman-in-the-dressing-room' superstition buster. He said yes, and it meant that I could be in the dressing room. I didn't thank him until later. I just moved with the wave and couldn't believe my luck.

Here in Africa, the dressing room is clean and antiseptic and viciously well-lit – aggressive movie star lighting. Clowns must put on their pancake in here, but I bet the clowns don't keep it at 85 degrees. There are two rooms really, separated by a bank of hot mirrors and open-arched doorways. I take up position at the make-up table (a foolish choice considering the heat), and wrap myself in a cloak of invisibility. Team Lewis goes to work. This is not a pious environment anymore than it is a crude one. The guys laugh and move about the room, unpacking things, preparing. They've got about two hours. Patrick starts up the music. Patrick, the concise Cockney, wearing his gray, shiny, double-breasted suit and purple tie, his gold Egyptian ring and his long, lean body. Patrick is in charge of music and running. He also deals with cars and seems to have more than his share of accidents. He'd had one on the freeways of Johannesburg. He said that the car in front of him blew a tire and part of it landed on the hood of the loaned white Mercedes. There was room for doubt. Tonight at 3.30, Patrick puts on the music.

Make no mistake, music is major. The music is planned, considered, rehearsed, censored, savored. The music is a vital and ever-present member of the team: gym, training, bedroom, dinner, cars and dressing room. I don't think Lennox could live without music. He lives *by* it. And now, he lies down with it, on his back, on a blue massage table. A buffed and oiled Lennox Lewis looks down on him from the posters taped to the walls. The music starts low – slow, heartbeat reggae. It's relaxed in here, joyful with anticipation, confident, as the Lion slumbers.

He's fast asleep in five minutes – lying on his back, his hands crossed peacefully over his chest, black sunglasses, white velour, and a pillow under his head. Scott takes position, standing near the champ's head. I lean back and stare at the painterly tableau: the Dread (as he's called during these days of 'Thunder in Africa') lying in state guarded by his mate. Later it will seem to have been too short a sleep. Too loud the early music, too many people moving in and out of the dressing room. Later, like Oswald and Ruby, I will think, 'Security was a little blasé there in the protective bowels. What was that driver doing in the dressing room, watching? Who were those people without names, wandering in and out?'

It's 4.00 a.m. in Johannesburg. The guys quiet down as they go about their business: Courtney cuts towels. He's a serious man, Courtney. His seriousness is his strength. Not too long from now, I will have an image seared into my head: Courtney, coming through the ropes. Courtney, bracing the risen, but fallen, hero against the ropes, holding him tight, straight up, in place, allowing the fact that it is over to sink in for Lennox, as Courtney holds him tight. These towels Courtney is cutting as Len sleeps, they'll be in the corner. They'll be used to wipe up the sweat. Mom washes them, a favorite detergent, no softener. It's all thought out. It's a science.

Manny sets up his wrapping office on the back of a chair. A towel is taped to the chair and tape is taped to the towel. Only Manny can wrap Len's hands, right hand always first. Manny is not happy. He hasn't been happy since he arrived in South Africa. He hasn't been happy since he *heard* about South Africa. Manny asked Lennox to get in the sauna tonight. A first. Lennox said no. Manny's request was Lennox's private premonition – Manny didn't feel good about the fight. Manny wasn't worried about Rahman. It had to mean that Manny didn't feel good about Lennox. Harold gaffer-tapes plastic water bottles for traction and ices them down. Ron runs swinging door interference – moving the sightseers, the ubiquitous not-yet-ready-for-visitor status loiterers out of the foyer. Now, HBO must be dealt with. Dignitaries are politely put off for a little while longer. And we listen to the music: 'Even though I walk through the valley of the shadow of death, this is the life that I choose.' It's really hot in here. 90 degrees, maybe. Ron stands beside Scott. Now there be two guards. Patrick turns the music just a little bit louder.

'If you ride like lightning, you'll crash like thunder.'

Suddenly, Len is awake. He speaks softly with Scott, who leans in to hear as the champ whispers from his prone position. A gaggle of VIPs enters; Len greets them on his back. Richard prepares the British flag for its entrance. Manny mixes up the cut solution. It hasn't been used very often. He won't use it tonight. Len will leave the ring without a scratch on him. Egerton Marcus, Lennox's perennial sparring partner, old buddy from Canada, Olympic silver medal winner, is trying really, really hard not to dance. Now, he's shadowboxing. Eggie's sweating. God, it's hot.

Len's arms are crossed over his chest now. He's meditating. Yes, he is. One day he asked me to teach him how to meditate. Yoga was out, but we could try meditation. He sat down beside me, lotus-crossed that long body as I, with excruciating self-consciousness, talked him through it. After we finished, I asked, 'How was that?'
   'Okay, but I was a little uncomfortable. My back hurt.'
   'No! If you hurt you say so, you move.'
   'I didn't want to interrupt you.'
   'But, you should.'
   'No, mon, I didn't want to. Anyway, I think I do this.'

People find their spaces. I am afraid to enter no-woman's land. Scott had said I could: 'It's a little like an elevator, you find your space.' But, he had also told me that our hotel compound outside Johannesburg was 'a little like Waco', so … I make my own decision. I'm offered a chair up closer, but I remain sitting high on my blue massage table in the anteroom. Harold departs for Rahman's room; somebody has to be present for his hand-wrapping and marking. I ask Courtney if he has to cut up any more towels. I'll help. Nope. He's done.

Prince is smiling. Prince, a real prince from Ghana. Lennox had begun calling Prince 'Casper', because of his beautifully shaped, round head. 'Who's this Casper?' Prince continually asks. No one will tell him. Earlier this week, Prince came to Lennox's hotel room to deliver some bit of business info and pat his friend and watch a little chess, and, as he left, he stopped at the door, put that round, lovable head back into the room, and said, with unlimited affection, 'Bye, Champ.' Prince Poku. Prince will wipe away tears before the evening is through, wipe them with a clean white handkerchief – a living portrait of a heartbroken man, hidden, he thought, from view. He will cry. Brief, but necessary. The handkerchief will be folded and returned to his pocket. He will ask me not to mention it to the guys.

And, they sing to the music, 'How does this sound so good, how does it sound so nice?'

He's up. The word spreads – he's up. He's shadowboxing in white velour and a black nylon do-rag. Lennox has a backwalking move which truly is that seldom seen 'poetry in motion'. Scott stays very close, still guarding. Ron is starting to sway, just a little bit. Ron, if truth were told, has the best moves in the room. He will stomp, he will shout – that quiet, impeccable, handsome man. He's saying a few soft words to the champ. I can't understand what he's saying, but he's making contact.

The checker, the man from Rahman's camp, enters, stands and waits. He is politely unobtrusive; no jibes, no eyeballs rolling, no sighs. He understands. He waits.

At 4:10 a.m. Lennox puts on his shoes, or rather, his shoes are put on him. Left first. His shoes are made especially for him. They read 'Slew 'em' and 'Fire' on the sides. Lennox is totally quiet, totally still. Black sunglasses, a stoic face, sitting, as Courtney ties up his shoes. I remember my first day at training camp, when I watched with amusement as these men hovered, and served, tied him up, wiped him down, dressed him, watered him, urged him, and praised him. Watch them now as it all comes together and they become one with the fighter and in silent and steady motion they meld into a living sculpture of grace and beauty, strength and determination. Here's what you learn – what they all know too well: they're a team, but only one man steps into the ring.

Patrick spins up the volume. The music is getting raw. I heard some wanton Hollywood gossip about a woman who was invited up to Len's own bedroom one night in London. She said, 'He played weird music.' Oh, the undeserving.

Manny is quiet, thinking. Is he excited, or is he nervous? 'The river is wide. The river is deep. There is a lot of milk and honey on the other side.'

Len strips down to the T-shirt. Manny begins the wrapping. Rahman's man steps closer. The music steps higher. I notice an old Afrikaner in a very shiny suit doing some bad dance moves in the corner. Who is *he*? A workingwoman in a headset comes in with a time notice. Quick, vibe alert! You can feel it. She's too loud, too hyper. Wrong. Get her out of here! Ron takes the job. I stay on my table, legs crossed under me. Okay, Jake the driver is in here. How the hell? But, he's cool. He's fine. He's watching, silently. It's all good. Blaise takes photos; he's the only man who could. Earlier that week, as Joe and I sat in a car, waiting, waiting for Blaise, I expected a little impatience on Joe's part. But, no. As Blaise came ambling along the sharp African lawn, seeing us, smiling, ambling on over, Joe had said, 'I'd give anything to be like Blaise. Look at him. He's never going to have a heart attack.'

Manny wraps the right hand first. I've seen this now many times, and it never ceases to amaze me. It's like watching a really great ironer. You know, a *great* ironer? Around the buttons, sides, back, end with the collar. Precise and neat, no corners hanging out, Lennox's knuckles are perfectly guarded with the little bit of extra foam he favors. What a responsibility. Only Manny wraps the hands. I read that Ali would have his hands numbed when need be. And Eggie, he fought his Olympic bout with a broken hand, but he never told. The Rahman man signs the wraps and leaves. Okay, Eggie is singing now, 'Your Majesty, I want to have a conversation with you.' And, the shirt comes off at 4.30 a.m.

Len's warming up, moving, bouncing. He's in his black underwear and, as the big red codpiece is strapped on, I politely move out of sight, back to the make-up table and the broiling lights. Sunglasses are OFF! The scarf is removed. That long twisted hair is already sewn up.

DREAD!

He's starting to sweat. He's beyond male, more than mere man, 'His Majesty'. Two days earlier, I sat on the grass with a few fellow lazy bums, and Lennox walked by in his white terry-cloth robe, en route to his physiotherapist's, Leigh McGuinness's, room for a massage. He gently patted a few of our heads as he moved all 6 feet 5 inches of himself gracefully across the green lawn. Blaise said it best, as our favorite pugilist passed by: 'He could be king here.' If the aliens come begging, and he's willing, I'd say, 'Send him! He's the best we have.' Send him to Mars, okay, but why did he have to come to this whorehouse on Venus?

Patrick shimmies over to the boom box to turn the music up LOUDER! Egerton shadowboxes alongside Lennox. Scott keeps his unblinking eyes on Len. Scott, still standing with his arms crossed, still guarding his man – he's in the zone. Where are you, Scott? What does it feel like to train with this man for eight weeks? Be willing to talk at 4.00 in the morning, play endless games of chess, wrestle and be trapped in that 84-inch stretch headlock. Be quiet and just take it – take the bitching and the crankiness – when you have to. Compete as an equal and fight to win, when you have to. Everybody's on their feet. Me, too. The tables are carried from the room. The chairs are out. The room is long and deep and empty but for those of us standing out of his way, and the champ is moving. Egerton feels it. He mimics every twist and turn, every rotating cup and sliding foot. Prince is laughing. We feel it too, God bless him. We all feel it, too.

All eyes are on Len. No talking. All eyes are feeding him, giving him our everything. Ministering to him. It's religious; I dare you to say it's not. I'm sweating. The room smells like boys. Boy spirit. Now Lennox is down on the floor, sitting on a beige woolen blanket I recognize as the hotel's. Courtney stretches him. Harold pours water into his mouth. The corner guys put on their white satin shirts. Frank Maloney, the manager – I've only met him once before at the Tua fight – gets into his flag suit. He's worn it at every fight for the past eleven years. Frank notices that there's a bloodstain on the pocket. And it's not Len's blood. I sit in my cloak of invisibility. That night, before the fight, I had dreamed of black baby animals – a black baby cat and a black baby tarantula. Young Blaise takes the picture.

Okay, we're seriously stretching now. Len wants his codpiece adjusted, laced tighter in the back. I step out. It's hotter. Grease him down, Courtney. The pre-fight is showing on the monitor in the dressing room. Len's stretching and watching. He gets up, moves, on his toes, shadowboxing. The guys move in and wipe up the floor, using those cut-up white towels, just like they always do, fast and neat. Don't let him slip, don't let him fall down. Len keeps moving, never pausing to check, knowing he is protected.

And the voices rise. 'Yeah! Champ-EE-on!' Clapping. The guys all gather at his side as Courtney stretches those long arms out behind. Longer, higher, further. The strings on his corset are taped down. The floor is wiped. Soon come. All that teamwork, all that practise. Soon come. The sweat rolls off the man, rolls over the grease on his back, down his arms. The smell. The heat. Voices rising. Music blaring. It's 4.50 in South Africa. We're under the big top.

The belts are readied. They're carried in metal suitcases (or sometimes tossed into duffel bags), three of them, red and green, heavy and gaudy, holding photos of past champions. The red gloves are tied on. It's hot. A hundred degrees? It will be 107 degrees in the ring, at 5.00 in the morning. Harold tapes the gloves. A few officials move in and out of the room. An official from the WBC comes in and signs the gloves with a black magic marker.

Ron shouts, 'CHAMP-*EEE*-ON!'

Lennox hits his hands together. That's one of his things, an entrance thing, fists hitting together. Mop the floor men. Manny puts on the mitts. Manny is actually blushing as Len blasts him with a few left jabs, big hits to the mitts. Manny offers a few tips. Courtney wipes up the sweat.

'WICKED!'

Len makes a 'Tsssssp' sound when he hits. Jab. Jab. Jab.

'SLEW 'EM!'

All those dread-heads, the black Rapunzels, dancing around the champ. It is all coming together, now. At 5.05 a.m.

Len looks at himself in the mirror.

'RASTA! LION!' He's stalking the cage.

Harold is talking softly, beginning to quiet it down – soothing, spiritual talk. Manny keeps the mitts on. The pre-fight is over. Len is watching himself on TV. He's knocking out Michael Grant, over and over again. 5.15 – the white satin boxers go on. Len holds his gloved and useless hands up over his head as the corner men pull up his pants. The floor is wiped. Len is wiped.

Now, the circle forms. Harold says the prayer. We all put our hands in, me and Jake the driver, too. 'Thank you God for bringing us to South Africa,' says Harold. 'Let there be no damage. No pain. Protect Lennox, protect Rahman.'

'Burn dem, the Olympic, World Champion! CHAMP-EEE-UUN!'

Patrick's got the belts. Out we go, down the corridor, into the lights, into the circus. I move out of the way, I follow, I lead – whatever. We encircle Lennox, protect him, allowing him to stay focused and dignified and feeling safe because he's going to war, man. Showbiz African warriors dance their way down the aisle, clearing the way ahead of us. We slip away, one by one, as the boxer and the corner team near the ring.

'Get up, stand up, stand up for your rights. Get up, stand up. Don't give up the fight.'

I'm separated from the others, trapped in the crowd and wind up in the wrong seat, in front of two sixty-year-old Chinese ladies in Mao suits. I look over the audience. I see no Africans. This is not what Lennox wanted. He wanted to bring the heavyweight bout to Africa, like Ali had. He'd visited Soweto, visited the AIDS orphanages, bused poor kids to the open sparring, carried a wreath into the memorial at Ellis Park Stadium to honor the 43 soccer fans who had tragically died there the previous week. He got shit for it in the press ('He should be training!'). At 5.00 in the morning the champion finds himself at a rich man's fight – five thousand seats, not a bad (or cheap) seat in the house – not a poor fight fan to be seen. This is not the fight he wanted.

'The Undisputed Heavyweight Champion of the World ... L-E-N-N-O-X L-E-W-I-S!'

Ron and Scott spot me and call me down to ringside. Blaise finds his space to shoot this damn cockfight and get the hell out of here. Prince and Mom, brother Dennis and Jake, the driver – God knows how he got into these seats – God bless him. And Leigh, and his pals, Kojack and Mark and Candace and Arun, Kamal, Bali, Julie, Kat and Lloyd, Will, and his first trainer, Arnie from Canada, who's already almost in tears, smiling, he's so proud of his boy. The fight begins and the corner team is crackling and he is winning. His eyes? His focus? He's moving slowly, oddly ('Keep your hands up, Lennox!'), but he's fighting his fight, and, as he says, absorbing the other man's energy. I admire him so. I love them all. The sweet scientist and those sweet Rapunzels and sweet trainers and sweet friends, so sweet, and everybody and everything that allows this sweet man to stand up and fight.

And then, he loses.

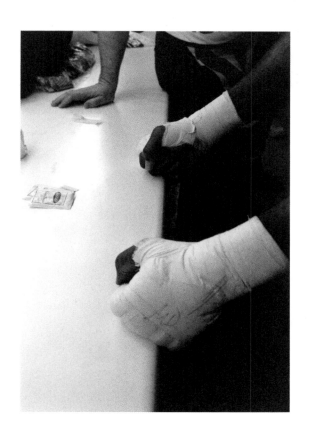

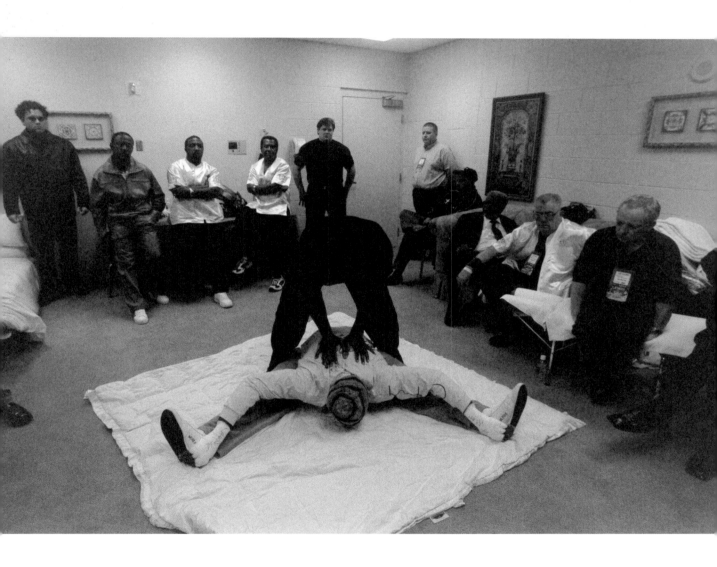

Lennox's Room

'What a buzz kill.' Scott DeMercado

We took the long way home. For better or worse, as the sun came up, the white mercenaries stuck to protocol and varied their route. It was the longest ride yet. By late afternoon, it was raining. Pouring, just as it had after Ali-Frazier. 'Thunder in Africa.' It smelled like Africa – an older, dustier earth seemingly refusing to turn to mud. We watched the storm coming and going from Lennox's room. Lennox had made it to his post-fight party in Johannesburg sometime around 1.00 p.m. After a shower and some phone calls, Lennox put on nice clothes and insisted we all get back into those white Mercedes and make one more trek across the plains. He stood silently, gallantly, by the front door of the restaurant and ushered his team and friends inside, as he waited for his mother. He escorted her into the celebration.

It was a tender party. The champagne flowed as freely as the tears. Lennox played DJ and got people up and dancing and laughing. He was unharmed. Finally, that was all that really mattered. I remembered one day in camp having asked Scott if there was anything I should watch out for – any taboo to observe, any words or actions to be avoided – so as not to twist the man up in any way. 'Give him more credit than that!' laughed Scott. 'You know what you're doing, don't you?' he asked me. 'You're trying to protect him. You just don't want to see him get hurt.'

Watching Lennox go down – it was heartbreak in slow motion. It wasn't the punch that hurt, it was watching that big body fall down. The head hit the floor. Oh, the sound of it. The face came up again. The eyes, dark and unfocused. And the terrible, gut-wrenching fear that he might be hurt. Hurt forever. No, he is fine. He remains unharmed.

I whisper, 'Was it my fault?', still unable to let go of that nagging superstition; he had allowed my presence as he prepared. Len's sitting on the couch, playing chess. He shakes his head no.

Thunder rips and roars. And then it's quiet, but for the rain on the roof. No one has left his side for more than a few minutes at a time during these odd hours as twilight descends; this out of time, when rightfully it should have been dawn.

'Hey, no one died here!' Patrick had shouted, back in the dressing room, as he slammed on the music. 'Nobody died here!'

Prince has the clicker. At one point, *Star Wars* comes on TV. Len lies draped across a chair, dozing, in a *mauve* velour leisure suit. There's a half-hearted, but full participation debate over the color of his Fubu (For Us By Us) pants and jacket. I call it violet, like his mother. Blaise calls it maroon. Lennox says 'yes and no' to all suggested hues, but he settles on mauve.

'What was his line?' Lennox asks, surprisingly, about my husband.

I try to remember.

'I don't think he had one. I think we both just felt we were meant to be together.'

Lennox nods. He waits, politely, through Harrison's first big scene in the alien bar, and then he says good night and goes to his room. Prince turns down the volume.

'Don't you hate it when somebody comes in and changes the music?' Eggie asks, as he does so. 'When somebody just comes in, and hey, nobody's complaining, but somebody just changes the music?'

I helped pack up his belongings the next day. He had moved into the city, into the fancy hotel. He was preparing to go on safari. There was a girl. In his bathroom, along with the vitamins and the Epsom salts and the clean, tidy effects of a cautious man, there was a Bible, lying open on the edge of the bathtub. He had read it before the fight. Isaiah 40:31. 'They that wait upon the Lord shall renew in their strength. They shall mount up with wings like an eagle. They shall run and not be weary. They shall walk and not faint.'

Interview #5
Summer, 2001

'I got hit. I went down. I took the count. It's boxing.

Winning and losing is the same to me. They're like yin and yang. Can't have one without the other. When it happened, the last moment I remember is looking at the ref. I'm getting up, I'm on my way up, and the ref jumps on me.

Then it dawned on me: he stopped it. So I thought, okay, I'm disappointed that this is actually happening to me. It's kind of embarrassing in one sense, you know. The best fighter in the world is suddenly knocked out. When this kind of thing happens, it always happens at the wrong time. It's supposed to happen in the gym when you're training and your sparring partner hits you, you go down, you get up okay, and then, you give it to him. This fucking guy caught me with this fucking punch? Why did this happen? Why would this have to happen today?

I wasn't allowed to get up. I felt the count was fast. I was confused on the mat, but, once I got up, I was fine. In order to get up, you need to get your faculties. So what do you do? What do you say? I suppose it's better to be safe this time and live to fight another day. I didn't like it. I'm a fighter. I've got a big heart. If I'm going to go out, mon, let me go out on my shield. Not being allowed to do that, it takes something from you.

For whatever reason it happened, it happened. We can look back. Manny can say there were weight problems. People can say I should've been there earlier. Some people would say it's Chinese astrology. Some say the number five – all these different excuses. You know, in a sense, I felt okay afterward. I felt a weight lifted off my shoulders. It was meant to happen for a reason. He's reignited the flame in me, now I've got something to prove, which makes it fresh for me. It's like I'm shooting a foul shot, which is the fight, yeah? Boom – I miss. I lose the fight. Do I go on or do I make this shot before I go on? You see? Let me make this shot first before I go on. See what I'm saying? Let me make this shot first.

I've already seen the future. My future is that I will get the rematch and I will win. And that's my aim. That's the future I want to create. I've seen that already. What comes between then and now, I'll just watch it all unfold. I know where I'm going to be.'

Contractually, there was to be an immediate rematch. But greedy hands and greedy hearts created a snafu. Rahman balked. Rahman left fourteen million on HBO's table and signed with Don King – twenty million pies in the sky and two hundred thousand cash packed neatly in a suitcase. Rahman carried that suitcase down the stairs and out of a Times Square hotel and back to Baltimore. There was a parade for the new champion, and another car accident. Past champions' portraits were pried out of the belts and new ones were inserted in their place. There would be a brand new Bentley in a Las Vegas parking lot, scores of newfound relatives dropping by, and some new diamond chains dangling around another muscular neck. There would be a scuffle on live TV and some serious name-calling. Mistakes were made. It was all tragically predictable. What happened? 'He went all ghetto fabulous on us,' says Lennox.

So, Lewis took Rahman to court. Don King and Cedric Kushner and Rahman himself piggybacked on the lawsuit – a cockfight on top of a cockfight. We all know it's a dirty business.

Rahman vs Lewis
November, 2001

Camp returned to the Poconos. Babies had been born: to Egerton, a girl, and Patrick, a girl. Blaise had a second son. Ron was expecting. Mom's beautiful granddaughter had come to live with her. Marissa – she was the joy of the season. Scott was engaged. Kojo was learning to swim and Lennox was falling in love.

In the second week of September, I sat with Lennox under a brilliant, empty sky in Central Park. New York City. He was due in camp on September 11, but neither he, nor anyone else, got where they were going during those unforgettable days.

'Are you ever afraid that you might kill someone in the ring?'

'No.'

I wish you could have seen him as he answered this question which I'd been waiting to ask. Everything that he *is* was so eloquent in that 'no': his experience, his skill, his faith, his simplicity, his honesty.

'Could you kill if you had to?'

'Yeah. Same as anybody.'

Team Lewis traveled to Las Vegas the second week of November. Lennox weighed in at 246 pounds. The odds were 5:1 Lewis the morning of the fight; by fight time, they were 2:1. Where was Lennox? He did no pre-fight press. His dressing room was closed. Locked. What was going on in there? Even Rahman came rumbling down the corridor, banging on Lennox's door, wondering what was going on in there. The Lion. Doing it his way. *His way* was going on in there.

That night, November 17, 2001?

Well, you know, you had to have been there.

Interview #6 the Poconos,
October, 2001

MM *So Lennox, you look great!*

Lennox gives me a look, indicating politely that I may tell him how great.

MM *Okay. So here's what I notice. Structural difference – you're very trim. You seem to be lifting from some other part of your body. You look two inches taller. There's a new gracefulness to you. Do you notice anything different?*

LL Not really. Just making sure I'm in good shape and box according to plan and give Rahman something that he hasn't seen before.

MM *Literally? Is there something new?*

LL Not really. Just trying to be more ... hit him with more speed in this fight. I'm just out to win. I'm the underdog. I'm actually boxing to get something that I lost. It's not a good position to be in, but, you know, I like being in this position.

MM *Do you? Why?*

LL Because a lot of people have doubts and it's up to me to prove them wrong. It's always sweeter winning in that sense.

MM *How's the fight going to go?*

LL The first two rounds are going to be kind of like feel-out rounds. I'm going to see what he's coming in with new. I'm going to try to make my presence known early, and keep him at the end of my jab. Definitely going to try to do a lot more jabs than in the first fight, and I'll stand a greater chance of being successful.

MM *Lennox Lewis's jab. Definition?*

LL Jabs are the key to everything. They start off everything. Before you can do any combinations you jab first. The jab is a defensive weapon and an offensive weapon, and noted in history as being one of the prime weapons of the boxer. I can knock someone out with it if I catch him correctly. I can bloody his nose, get in the eyes. And, I'm picking up points while I use it. You know Muhammad Ali made the jab very famous. It's a weapon that's always in your face – it's a pest.

MM *You didn't use it so much in the last fight.*

LL Didn't use it as much as I should have. It's funny because that's my prime weapon and when I move away from it, things always seem to fall apart.

MM *What do you think Rahman's game plan is going to be?*

LL I think he's going to try to stay low. Try to get inside to my body. The normal things boxers always try to do. Holyfield, one of the most gifted boxers, tried to do the same thing and was unsuccessful.

MM *Try to get inside on you?*

LL Yeah. And try to work my body and try to slow me down. Rahman believes he's got a better jab than I do, and better punches, but you know, I don't think so.

MM *Prediction?*

LL I think the fight's going to go well on my side. I'm just going to outfight him and outclass him and win on points.

MM *You're not going for a knockout?*

LL It's funny, when I go in there trying to knock the person out, it never comes. And when I go in there not anticipating a knockout, it always comes. So anything can happen, and I'm quite happy to win on points.

MM *Which song are you going to play when you come in?*

LL James Brown, 'Big Payback'.

MM *What happens after this?*

LL This fight? There's a big fight with Mike Tyson out there, you know. What the world wants to see – the Mike Tyson/Lennox Lewis fight – and what I hope to give them.

MM *Did you watch Tyson's fight the other night? What did you think?*

LL I thought that only one guy was fighting. He wasn't up against any opposition. He did look okay, in the mental sense; he seemed pretty serene and not the mad Tyson that everybody had expected. He went about his work the way he should have. I would like to see him against someone that actually throws some punches and hits him – see how he deals with getting hit.

MM *So, Tyson just moves in and moves in. And that's how he'd fight you?*

LL Right.

MM *How would you counter that?*

LL Just give him something to worry about. I catch him as he's coming in because he's only got one thing to do and that's to come in. Maybe even try to back him up.

MM *Has he got endurance?*

LL I don't think he has endurance, because you know he started to slow down after the fourth round. I start to pick it up as I play. Tyson's a guy you have to bring into the deep end and watch him fall apart, because that's what will definitely happen.

MM *So what happens after that? In six months you've got your belts, you've fought Tyson...*

LL Retired.

MM *You've retired. Then what?*

LL Then think about another goal that I want to accomplish and go do that.

MM *Have you got that planned?*

LL No.

MM *Does it worry you?*

LL No.

MM *Imagine what you'll be like when you're fifty.*

LL Oh. Fifty years old. Hopefully, I'll have a nice family with business interests to keep me busy. Probably, a young student. Teaching him boxing.

MM *Would you like to have somebody you're bringing along?*

LL Absolutely. I find myself doing that now to anybody who'll listen. Teaching and showing different things to save them time, because I realize having that in my corner when I was going through life as a boxer helped me as well. I'd be a great trainer.

MM *Are most boxers willing to train as hard as you do?*

LL Umm…

MM *Describe yourself as a boxer right now.*

LL I'm more defined now. More seasoned than before. Ten years ago I was young, strong, fast, vibrant. I'm all of that today, but more seasoned. I've got more brainpower, which is more important in boxing than brawn. Ten years ago I had more brawn and maybe less brain. I get more aches and pains than when I was younger. Endorphins don't kick in as much as when I was younger.

MM *How are you taking care of your body?*

LL I'm eating more raw foods, organic foods.

MM *Do you feel a difference?*

LL Yeah. I mean it's funny. Subtle. My barber says he sees it in my hair. Eating some coconuts. Drinking coconuts.

MM *What does that do for you?*

LL It gives me that 'island thing' lacking in our … what do you call this kind of society?

MM *Urban?*

LL Yeah. Urban society.

MM *So, Lennox, this fight coming up. It is…?*

LL Trivial.

MM *Is it redemptive?*

LL Yes.

MM *Is it revengeful?*

LL Yes.

MM *Is it personal?*

LL To a certain degree, yes.

MM *Is it climactic?*

LL Yes.

MM *Is it melancholy?*

LL Define?

MM *Bittersweet.*

LL Yes.

MM *Knowing that once again, win or lose, it might be the last time?*

LL Yes. The 'last hurrah' kind of thing.

MM *It's interesting.*

LL Yah, mon.

MM *Life is beautiful, huh? You're lucky to have this hiccup little fight.*

LL Yah, mon.

MM *Hey, 'yes-and-no' man, I got no nos. Thank you, Mister Lewis.*

LL No problem.

Brutal?

Yes and no.

Statistics

Born: London, England
                    September 2 1965

Heavyweight: 246 pounds

Height: 6 feet 5 inches

Style: Orthodox

International honors

World Junior Champion 1983

World Cup Champion 1983

Commonwealth Gold 1986

Olympic Gold 1988

European Heavyweight Champion 1990

British Heavyweight Champion 1991

Commonwealth Heavyweight Champion 1992

WBC Heavyweight Champion of the World 1993 and 1997

WBC Heavyweight Champion of the World 1999

WBA Heavyweight Champion of the World 1999

IBF Heavyweight Champion of the World 1999

IBO Heavyweight Champion of the World 1999

Linear Undisputed Heavyweight Champion of the World 2000

BBC Sports Personality of the Year 1999

Awarded the CBE December 2001

Fight record

Date	Opponent	Win/Draw/Loss	Result
27 June 1989	Al Malcolm	W	KO
21 July 1989	Bruce Johnson	W	TKO
25 September 1989	Andy Gerrard	W	TKO
10 October 1989	Steve Garber	W	KO
5 November 1989	Melvin Epps	W	DSQ
18 December 1989	Greg Gorrell	W	TKO
31 January 1990	Noel Quarless	W	KO
22 March 1990	Calvin Jones	W	KO
14 April 1990	Mike Simwelu	W	KO
9 May 1990	Jorge Dascola	W	KO
20 May 1990	Dan Murphy	W	TKO
27 June 1990	Ossie Ocasio	W	PTS
11 July 1990	Mike Acey	W	TKO
31 October 1990	Jean Chanet	W	TKO
6 March 1991	Gary Mason	W	TKO
12 July 1991	Mike Weaver	W	KO
30 September 1991	Glen McCrory	W	KO
21 November 1991	Tyrell Biggs	W	TKO
1 February 1992	Levi Billups	W	PTS
30 April 1992	Derek Williams	W	KO
11 August 1992	Mike Dixon	W	TKO
31 October 1992	Donovan Ruddock	W	KO
8 May 1993	Tony Tucker	W	PTS
1 October 1993	Frank Bruno	W	TKO
6 May 1994	Phil Jackson	W	KO
24 September 1994	Oliver McCall	L	TKO
13 May 1995	Lionel Butler	W	KO
2 July 1995	Justin Fortune	W	TKO
7 October 1995	Tommy Morrison	W	TKO
10 May 1996	Ray Mercer	W	PTS
7 February 1997	Oliver McCall	W	TKO
12 July 1997	Henry Akinwande	W	DSQ
4 October 1997	Andrew Golota	W	KO
28 March 1998	Shannon Briggs	W	TKO
26 September 1998	Zeljko Mavrovic	W	PTS
13 March 1999	Evander Holyfield	D	
13 November 1999	Evander Holyfield	W	PTS
29 April 2000	Michael Grant	W	KO
15 July 2000	Frans Botha	W	TKO
11 November 2000	David Tua	W	PTS
22 April 2001	Hasim Rahman	L	KO
17 November 2001	Hasim Rahman	W	KO

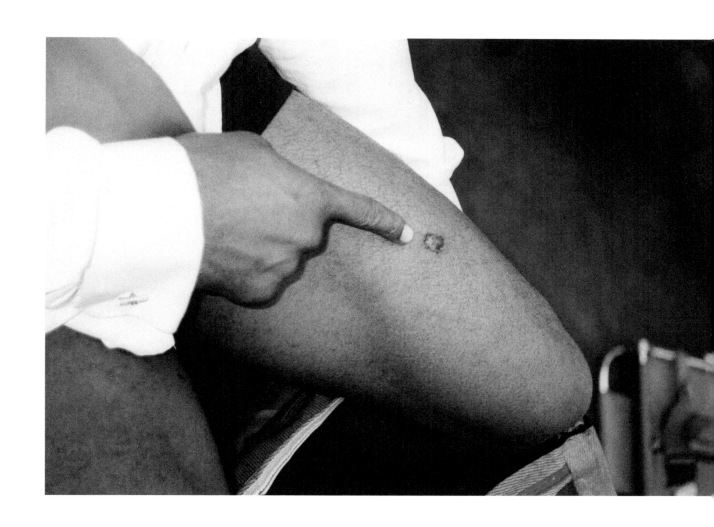

Photographs

Lennox Lewis is three time Heavyweight Champion of the World. An Olympic gold medal winner, he has been boxing professionally for 13 years. He'd like to thank his fans worldwide. "This is me, chillin'. This is me, keepin' it sweet."

Blaise Hart lives in Jamaica. He has documented the career of his friend Lennox Lewis for the past six years. He thanks the Team for all the good times. He'd like to acknowledge his teacher Silvia Lizama, Charles Meaden, his wife Tammy and family.

Melissa Mathison works as a screenwriter (*E.T.*, *Kundun*). This is her first book. She'd like to thank Lennox Lewis and his extended Team for their gracious participation in the writing of this book. She thanks her family and, of course, Blaise.